PRAISE FO̶ ̶ ̶ ̶ ̶ ̶ ̶ ̶ ̶ IE

A Los A̶ ̶ ̶ ̶ ̶

"A searingly honest account…written with all the energy of a twenty-first century Woodward and Bernstein."

—*Dazed & Confused*

"*News Junkie* is an admirably honest piece of work."

—*The Portland Mercury*

"Jason Leopold's *News Junkie*, an autobiographical look at Leopold's accidental entrance into journalism, is a powerful piece that delves into one man's misery and success."

—*Boston Herald*

"Leopold, one of the reporters who broke the Enron story, is now breaking his own story: How he got addicted to cocaine, committed grand theft, cleaned himself up, and found happiness as a 'news junkie.' This scrappy memoir…might become required reading for aspiring journalists."

—*Publishers Weekly*

"With its superbly presented candor, *News Junkie* is very highly recommended reading both as a memoir offering unique insights into the mind and life of an investigative journalist, and as a 'slice of life' window into the stories and personalities behind headline stories of corruption and crime."

—*Midwest Book Review*

"Investigative superstar Jason Leopold spares no one, least of all himself, in this devastatingly accurate first-hand exposé. *News Junkie* provides the best account so far of how, and why, current American journalism has become so pharisaical, spineless, and detached from the truth."

—T. D. Allman, journalist and author of *Finding Florida*

News Junkie

by Jason Leopold

A Vireo Book | Rare Bird Books
Los Angeles, Calif.

THIS IS A GENUINE VIREO BOOK

A Vireo Book | Rare Bird Books
453 South Spring Street, Suite 531
Los Angeles, CA 90013
rarebirdbooks.com

Set in Minion
Printed in The United States
Distributed in the US by Publishers Group West

10 9 8 7 6 5 4 3 2 1

Publisher's Cataloging-in-Publication data

Leopold, Jason.
    News Junkie / by Jason Leopold.
    p. cm.
    ISBN 978-1-940207-23-0
    Revised edition.

1. Leopold, Jason. 2. Journalists—Biography. 3. Journalism—United States—
History—21st century. 4. Press—United States—History—21st century. 5. Enron
Corp—Corrupt practices. 6. Drug abuse. 7. Journalistic ethics. I. Title.

PN4738 .A38 .L46 2014
071/.471/092—dc23

For Lisa: My wife, best friend, and soul mate
who always wanted me to be honest with myself

INTRODUCTION

You gain strength, courage and confidence by every experience in which you really stop to look fear in the face. You are able to say to yourself, "I have lived through this horror. I can take the next thing that comes along." You must do the thing you think you cannot do.

—Eleanor Roosevelt

A N "ORGY OF DISCLOSURE." That's how the journalist, Jason Fagone, characterized *News Junkie* in a profile he wrote about me. "It feels like the outpouring of a guy who realizes he's been destroyed by the secrets he's kept and vows to never keep one again."

It's true. *News Junkie* is a book I needed to write. Everyday, I would wake up and try to expose the secrets of some corrupt politician or corporate executive. Yet, I was haunted by my own dark secrets. I felt like a hypocrite and a fraud.

So yeah, I purged myself of feelings of guilt and shame in the pages of my memoir. I confronted my demons. I was brutally honest. It was the only way I could tell my story.

I wanted you to *feel* the adrenaline rush when I landed my first scoop. I wanted you to *experience* the metamorphosis after I snorted my first line of cocaine. When I was at my lowest point, standing on the George Washington Bridge, looking over the side of the railing into the Hudson, I wanted you to *understand* why I seriously considered jumping. When I met my wife, Lisa, I wanted you to *see* my soul mate.

I thought breaking my own story would finally set me free. I thought it would be my path to redemption. But I fucked it all up.

The first edition of *News Junkie* was published in May 2006—right around the time I erroneously reported that George W. Bush's former deputy chief of staff, Karl Rove, had been indicted by a federal grand jury over his role in the unauthorized disclosure of a covert CIA operative's identity. I had been writing about the Valerie Plame affair for more than two years and, after speaking with FBI sources I had cultivated, believed I scored an exclusive. I rushed to publish a story based entirely on anonymous sources. My colleagues in the media pilloried me when the case was closed with Karl Rove escaping a perp walk.

It did not help my cause that I wrote a book and revealed that I was a convicted felon, recovering drug addict and alcoholic, liar, and thief at the same time I had asserted, without so much as a single caveat, that one of the most powerful men in politics was going to be prosecuted. It didn't help my cause that the story I wrote was published on a website called *TruthOut*. It didn't help my cause that I had repeated the same exact mistakes I had copped to in *News Junkie*, which I vowed never to repeat again.

I paid dearly for botching that story. It cost me my credibility. Karl Rove called me a "nut with Internet access" in his own memoir, *Courage and Consequence*.

I've spent the past eight years methodically rebuilding my trustworthiness as an investigative journalist. Instead of relying on anonymous sources, I use the government's most coveted documents (which I obtain through the Freedom of Information Act) to break news.

During the course of my reporting, I stumbled upon a family secret that had been concealed from me. It explained why I have been compelled throughout the course of my two-decade long career to chase down secrets. The remarkable and disturbing discovery forms the basis for the next installment of my memoir.

I realize that I left a lot of carnage behind and *News Junkie* does not address the people who trusted me whom I have hurt. To you, I sincerely apologize and ask for your forgiveness.

I've changed since I wrote my memoir. I'm a father now. I can finally look back at my life and say that all of this shit I carried around for so many years is truly in the past. Good riddance. But this book is about the choices that I made before that realization. This is the story of what my life *used* to be like. This is what it was like to live inside of my skin. This is what it felt like to be a news junkie.

—*Jason Leopold, July 2014*

NEWS JUNKIE

ONE

I GUESS YOU COULD SAY I was lucky. Maybe I was in the right place at the right time. Perhaps some higher power was looking out for me. Whatever the explanation, something made me call Steve Maviglio one Sunday afternoon in July 2001.

Maviglio had been Governor Gray Davis' press secretary for nearly a year and was miserable. He hadn't had a girlfriend in three years and people were beginning to question whether he was heterosexual. He was forty-two years old and lived alone in Sacramento with his cat, Enzo.

His job was to make the governor look good by any means necessary, and Maviglio considered himself gifted at turning a bad situation into a positive news story. The lonely bachelor despised reporters, particularly those who called him only for information. His primary nemesis was a feisty reporter for *The Wall Street Journal*, Rebecca Smith. Whenever Smith called Maviglio for a comment, she'd push his buttons with, "Can't you do better?" or "Is that really what you want to say?" I would see Maviglio turn beet red, veins popping out of his pockmarked forehead, when he was on the phone with Rebecca.

Maviglio and I, however, got along quite well. I genuinely liked the guy. He could count on me for a good laugh. At least once a day I would send him e-mails making fun of the governor or the other reporters. We were both transplanted East Coasters. I'm from the Bronx. He grew up in New Jersey, a total Guido. When we reminisced about East Coast cuisine, I discovered that Maviglio had a soft spot for hot pastrami on rye, so I surprised him with one when he was holed up in the governor's Los Angeles office doing damage control on the energy crisis.

I spoke to Maviglio more than any of my other sources. It made me feel important to say that Governor Gray Davis' press secretary was a friend. When Maviglio flew to Los Angeles, I would pick him up at the airport and comp his meal on my Dow Jones American Express card. Most of the time Maviglio seemed depressed and sounded robotic, never showing any sign of excitement. I always felt the need to cheer him up.

And though I made him feel comfortable enough, Maviglio kept secrets about the energy crisis close to the vest. When it came down to it, he knew that I was a journalist first and a friend second, and that I might sell him out for the price of a good pastrami sandwich.

When I phoned Maviglio that fated Sunday afternoon I was jonesing for a story. He answered on the first ring.

"Yo, motherfucker."

"What's up?"

"What's wrong this time?" I said. "You in need of an escort?"

Suddenly he asked, "What do you know about this investigation by the SEC?"

Oh yeah, the Securities and Exchange Commission investigation. Bill Jones, a Republican secretary of state and a fierce critic of Governor Davis, wrote a letter to the SEC insisting on an investigation into the governor's energy consultants buying stock in energy companies during contract negotiations.

When power utilities ran out of cash in 2001, California went through a half-dozen blackouts. Eventually, the state had to assume the role of buying electricity. The consultants' job was to convince the energy companies to sign long-term contracts with the state so that further blackouts were prevented.

Maviglio's voice sounded strange that Sunday. I sensed he was worried, so I tried bluffing him about my knowledge of state affairs.

"Well, the SEC is seriously looking into the issue."

"How do you know that?"

"Jones' office told me. They got a response from the SEC saying so. In fact, I am going to write a story about it."

"Any idea who they would be investigating?"

"Everyone and their mother."

"Did Jones' office give you any names?"

"Yeah, but I can't tell you."

"Come on, asshole."

"Anyone who bought stock in energy companies during the negotiations."

Due to the fact I was a business reporter with experience dealing with government agencies, Maviglio bought my bogus SEC tale hook, line, and sinker. Then it hit me.

"Steve, did you buy stock in any energy companies?"

"Off the record?"

"Sure."

"Yeah."

Jesus H. Christ. I just hit the jackpot.

"During the negotiations?" I asked.

"Yeah."

"Which ones?"

"Calpine."

"How much?"

"About twelve thousand dollars."

Maviglio also said he owned some Enron stock, but that he bought it in 1998. No matter when he bought it, it still made him look tainted.

If the SEC discovered that Maviglio invested in Calpine and was speaking publicly about the company in a way that boosted its stock price, it would appear as if he had an ulterior motive to increase his own financial stake.

Maviglio was present during contract negotiations and knew which companies were signing contracts with the state, for how much, and for how long. He admitted to me that he never filled out the financial disclosure form that everyone who works in state government is supposed to complete before they're hired. The form is also supposed to be turned in every year. Because Jones was making a stink about consultants failing to complete the paperwork, Governor Davis instructed his staff to dot the i's and cross the t's on all the financial disclosure forms so that his political enemies were deprived of attack ammunition. Once Maviglio turned in his disclosure form, it would be evident that he bought Calpine stock during contract negotiations, and would lose his job as a result. Davis had already fired five consultants who were heavily invested in a company that signed a contract with the state.

The energy crisis was spiraling out of control, and Gray Davis had already accused Enron of ripping off California, calling the corporate hierarchy "snakes" and "robber barons." California's Attorney General Bill Lockyer told a *The Wall Street Journal* reporter he would like to see Enron's CEO Ken Lay get raped in prison.

A week earlier I asked Maviglio why the governor was spewing venom at all the other energy companies but left Calpine unscathed. Davis had even posed with Calpine's CEO Pete Cartwright for a photo that ran in several newspapers. If the SEC found out that Maviglio had invested in Calpine and was grooming the company publicly, the conflict of interest would appear, to put it mildly, inappropriate.

"Dude, you're fucked. Big time."

"Thanks, asshole. Like I don't know that already."

"Why the fuck did you do something so stupid?"

"Because everyone told me it was a good investment and that I could make a lot of money."

"You're going to jail"

"Fuck you. You better not write about this. Everything I told you is off the record. The only people that know about this are you, my broker, and my lawyer."

Why Maviglio suddenly decided to confide in me I'll never know, but there was no way in hell that I was going to zip my lips on this bombshell story. I immediately phoned Andrew Dowell, my Dow Jones Newswires editor, at his New Jersey home. I always called Andrew on weekends, and I'm sure his wife hated me for it. Whenever I called, they'd be out to dinner, or in bed. But journalism isn't a nine-to-five occupation. If you get a call from your editor saying you have to cover a story, you can't say, "It's not my shift."

"Drew, it's Jason."

"What's up, dude?"

"Am I disturbing you? Are you in the middle of something?"

"We're eating dinner, but what's up?"

"You are not going to believe what I just found out. I was on the phone with Maviglio and we were talking about this whole

SEC crap that Jones sparked, and I asked him if he invested in energy companies and he said, 'Yes.' That he invested in them during the negotiations."

"Holy shit! Which ones?"

"Calpine and he owns some Enron stock, too, but he said he bought the Enron in ninety-eight."

"What a fucking idiot! Dude, you're amazing. Tell me about the conversation you had with him."

"Well, here's the problem. He told me everything off the record."

"What! He can't do that. Call him back and tell him you have to report it."

"I can't. I'll lose him as a source."

"Dude, you have to report this major story. Davis is trying to make it look like his consultants didn't do anything wrong. These guys are buying stock using inside information. That's criminal."

"I know,"

"So what are you going to do?"

"Let me work on him. I mean, we wouldn't be putting this out on the wire today right?"

"Nah, no one's around. But we should definitely put it out tomorrow."

"Okay."

"Good work, dude."

"Thanks."

◇

THE OFF-THE-RECORD RULE IN journalism is one of those unwritten agreements journalists make with their sources. Like a handshake. But there's no law that says if you print anything off the record you'll go to jail. It just means that your sources will distrust you and it makes the job of getting information far more difficult. There comes a time when a decision must be made on how far you're willing to go to get the story. I decided then that I was willing to cross ethical boundaries and risk my relationship with a key source to use what Maviglio revealed to me "off-the-record."

I'm not a unique case in the history of journalism. Reporters routinely cut corners for a juicy story. I'm not looking for a way to excuse my behavior. I'm just saying that it happens more often than you might think. All journalists have their own set of personal rules, and some actually take them seriously. They're the ones who slam on the brakes when a traffic signal changes from green to yellow. Others like me speed up and race through the intersection before the light turns red.

There is no feeling like breaking a news story. The only thing that comes close is when you snort that first line of coke and all insecurities vanish and you feel like you can conquer the world. The first time I felt that white powder trickle down my throat, everything in my life became perfect. Suddenly I was taller, better looking, and the pain of being rejected by my parents disappeared. High on coke, I could talk for hours with total strangers, and was no longer afraid of being rejected by women. Everyone was my friend. It was love at first sniff.

For years I tried chasing the feeling of that first high. The pathetic thing is that it never came back, and I nearly destroyed myself and my loved ones in pursuit of it.

Somehow I managed to keep myself employed and even moved up the ranks at several news organizations as a full-blown junkie and alcoholic. There were times when I would go cold turkey for a month or two, but then I would start the drinking and drugging all over again. I even tried to OD one night by snorting one impossibly big fat line. My heart raced so fast that I was convinced it was going to burst through my chest or shut itself down—but the fucker kept on ticking. Worst of all were those high hours of extreme paranoia, when I feared that rats were in my underwear and were going to crawl up my body and chew my face off. I'd strip off my clothes and stand naked in my bedroom, swatting at my genitals. This drug-induced terror was worse than death.

After enduring this sort of behavior for an entire year, my wife Lisa finally came to the conclusion that I was going insane. Incredible as it sounds, I managed to hide my addiction from her. Lisa is what drug addicts call a normie. She's never been drunk, never experimented with drugs. She couldn't spot a drug addict if he was sleeping right next to her. The quality of Lisa's innocence attracted me to her, and I thought she could save me from myself. Deep down I wanted to be like her, but I enjoyed being out of control and self-destructive. When Lisa could no longer deal with my psychotic episodes, she visited a therapist who told her that she was living with a drug addict. We went to see this therapist together, and the next thing I know Lisa's crying and telling me she knows I'm on drugs and that if I don't get help that she's going to divorce me. Of course, I denied everything and walked out. My first instinct was to jet to some other state where I could hide out—alone, with my drugs.

Then I had what addicts call a moment of clarity and walked two miles to my mother-in-law's house, knocked on the door and with my last bit of hope pleaded, "Help me."

I chose to ask my mother-in-law for help because she treated me like her own flesh and blood. It was nothing like the stereotypical in-law relationship portrayed in books or movies. We were friends. She knew everything about me, or so she thought.

Still, I was sure that when the dust settled she and everyone else in Lisa's family would judge me, just like my blood relatives judged me. My father always compared me, particularly my intelligence, to the other children in our neighborhood, who apparently were all geniuses.

On my wedding day, my father asked me if Lisa knew everything about me, all the sordid tales of my life. I said, "Yes, she knows everything."

"Wow. I don't think I would be so accepting if Michelle brought someone like you home," my father said, referring to my sister. That's when I stopped speaking to my parents. It was either that or commit suicide. My father's words made me doubt myself and wonder what my wife saw in me.

A bed was reserved for me at the rehab clinic and my mother-in-law and her sister, a psychoanalyst, drove me there. When I arrived, I was interviewed by a doctor who asked:

"Did you do cocaine last night?"

"Yes."

"How much?"

"I don't know. Two, three grams."

"Do you smoke?"

"No."

I smoked like a fiend but never in front of people. My mother-in-law was sitting in the chair next to me and I didn't want her to know that I smoked. Here I was admitting that I ingested a shitload of cocaine, but denied being a smoker because I was afraid of what my mother-in-law might think.

This was the same rehabilitation clinic in Marina Del Rey in which Kurt Cobain was confined the day before he escaped, flew back to Seattle, and blew his brains out. My rehab began like Cobain's, through intervention. And like Cobain, I hated myself and wanted to die.

After a month in that clinic I went home and have been sober ever since. I attend Alcoholics Anonymous meetings regularly. But I replaced my addiction to drugs and alcohol with an addiction to breaking news stories. Once you get a taste of the notoriety and the incredible feeling of power that come from breaking news, there is nothing else like it. Even in sobriety, I behaved like a drug addict. Instead of trying to cop a gram of coke, I was now hounding sources to see if they had any good scoops.

The anticipation of getting a news story, of being the first one to uncover a major development or a top-secret document, made my legs twitch and teeth chatter just like when I would be close to scoring an eight ball of coke. My sources were now my dealers, and I called them whenever the high from breaking a previous story was beginning to wear off.

I woke up at 7:00 a.m. Monday morning, showered, got dressed, and headed to a coffee shop. This was my morning routine. The only way I was able to work and stay high-strung was with my quadruple macchiato. Four shots of espresso in my stomach and pow—I was a freight train. The reason I got along so well with the French when visiting Paris was that I drank more coffee and smoked more cigarettes than they could. I only knew five French words and I would repeat them over and over: "*Un café, s'il vous plaît.*"

The Dow Jones Newswire Los Angeles bureau, of which I was chief, was only two miles from my house. The bureau housed two other reporters and was not your typical newsroom. It was a small space—one room to be exact—no bigger than a studio apartment in Manhattan. But we had an amazing view of the Hollywood sign from the fifteenth floor of the Wilshire Boulevard high-rise. Three large file cabinets and two dividers separated me from the other two reporters. Some genius thought that putting dividers in a 300-square-foot office would invite a level of privacy, but I could tell you everything that went on in my fellow reporters' lives.

Because Monday was going to be a big news day, I needed to get pumped up. I turned on the CD player in my car and cranked up Slayer's *Seasons in the Abyss*. The combination of strong coffee and heavy metal was like a shot of instant adrenaline. I felt mean. I clenched my teeth, looked in the rearview mirror, and made a mean face like the Mafia figures I admired. I lit a cigarette and sucked it down to the filter. After rehab, I kicked the drugs but still couldn't stop smoking.

Jessica, the other reporter who covered energy, got to the office an hour after me. She had just graduated from a journalism school in Texas and this was her first real reporting gig. Unlike most neophyte reporters I've worked with, Jessica had passion. I think she fed off of me. I told her the whole story about Maviglio buying stock in Calpine during the contract negotiations and she was floored.

"Shit, man, I wish I got that story."

"You wanna work on it with me?" I offered.

"Hell yeah!"

I figured that having another reporter on the story would serve two purposes: one, it would take some of the heat off because I could pass the buck to Jessica and make her call Maviglio for a comment; and two, it would show my superiors in New York that I wasn't one of these reporters who refused to share a byline.

I told Jessica we needed to figure out how to report this story without having me call Maviglio and tell him to come clean.

"Too bad Bill Jones doesn't know about it." Jessica said. "You know he would immediately put out a press release on this."

The last thing I wanted was for anyone else to get this story, and Jones had this terrible habit of using the *Los Angeles Times* to break stories. I hate that—politicians using the biggest newspapers to pimp their own agenda and deprive everyone else in the press a fair shot at the same story. I wasn't going to let that happen.

I figured a way to use Jones to help me report the scandal. I told Jessica to write the story as if we were going to send it out on the wire. Then I told her to be ready for my call.

On a traffic-clogged drive to a noon haircut appointment, my brain was seething with the story's repercussions. The public had a right to know that the Davis administration was padding pockets as a result of their knowledge of the energy crisis. Fuck worrying about violating journalism's code of ethics, I rationalized. The story was too fucking big.

On the barber chair, I called Bill Jones' Communications Director.

"Beth, hi, it's Jason Leopold with Dow Jones. I need you to do something for me. It's going to really benefit Jones."

"Oh yeah?"

"What I am about to tell you is highly confidential and I don't want you to let anyone know that it came from me."

"What is it?" she said, almost whispering.

"Steve Maviglio bought stock in Calpine during the contract negotiations. He also owns stock in Enron. He was in on the talks with the generators and he bought about 12,000 dollars worth of stock in Calpine afterward. He hasn't handed in his form that says what his financial holdings are, but I want you to call the *Sacramento Bee* and leak this story to them."

"Jason, this is really big. Are you sure about this?"

"Yes. I spoke to Steve yesterday and he told me this off the record. I need to report this story. I want you to tell the *Bee* that you found out from a mole in Davis' office that he bought the stock and hasn't told anyone in the state yet."

"Oh my God. He should be in jail. What he did is…"

"Listen, Beth, I'm on a deadline here."

"Okay."

"After you call the *Bee* I want you to call Jessica Berthold in my office and tell her the exact same thing you told the Bee. But don't tell her you spoke with me."

"Why?"

"Because that's how I'm going to break this story."

Then I phoned a Republican energy industry source and made him all hot and bothered with the Maviglio story, asking him to leak it to the *Los Angeles Times*.

I chose the *Bee* and the *Times* because the Sacramento newspaper champions itself as being ahead of the curve on political scandals, and the *Times* is so slow and methodical that they'd give Maviglio the impression that they'd been looking into his stock purchases for weeks. Both papers wouldn't be able to report my discovery until the following day, but the wire service I worked for could break it immediately. Voila, the story would be sent out to the top newspapers and half a million subscribers, and I'd get credit for reporting it first.

This was the most fulfilling haircut of my life, and I didn't even bother looking at the result. It hadn't even been twenty minutes since I asked Beth to spill to the *Bee*, but already I received an urgent voicemail.

"Leopold, it's Maviglio—I need you to call me NOW!"

My heart started racing. I didn't want to call him. I gripped the steering wheel as tight as I could until I felt pain in my knuckles. I tore the cuticles off my fingers with my teeth until my fingers started to bleed. Now I felt alive. It brought me back to my childhood, when I was about to get hit by my father. I knew I had to speak to Maviglio, otherwise he would know for sure that I was the source of the leak. I practiced my greeting out loud. I wanted to make sure I sounded like I had no idea what was going on. I punched the steering wheel and dialed his number at the governor's office pressroom. He answered right away.

"Hey... What's up?"

"I'm going to fucking kill you. You told the *Sacramento Bee* about me."

To avoid beatings at the hands of my father, it had paid to be defensive and at least sound like I was telling the truth.

"Are you out of your mind? What the fuck are you talking about? I never spoke to anyone at the Bee. I hate those bastards."

"Well, I just got a call from the *Sacramento Bee* and they said that Jones' office told them that I bought stock in Enron and Calpine. The only people I told about that are you, my lawyer, and my broker."

"Dude, think about this for a second. How would it benefit me if I told the *Sacramento Bee*? That makes no sense. Did you tell anyone in your own office about this?" I asked.

"The press office knows, but that's it."

"Any chance anyone there would have said anything?"

"No fucking way. I don't know how the fuck Jones could've found out. This is fucked. Now I have to go to the Governor and fucking tell him about this. I really hope you didn't say anything because if I lose my job I'm gonna kill you."

"Come on, dude. First of all, you know Jones is on a rampage and he has connections at the SEC."

Maviglio slammed the phone down. Back at the office, Jessica was a nervous wreck. She said she got a call from Beth at Jones' office that the *Sacramento Bee* and the *Times* were running Maviglio stories in the next day's paper.

"Relax. I leaked the story to Jones."

"You what?" There was disgust in her voice.

"Look, we needed to report this story. Sometimes the public good outweighs everything else. Maviglio never should have told me this off the record." I was lying. I didn't give two shits about the public good. At least not then. I simply sensed a big splash and wanted to boost my career and my ego.

"Well, what should we do now?" asked Jessica.

"I want you to call Maviglio and tell him that you got a call from Jones' office about him buying shares in Calpine and Enron. I want you to ask him how much he bought, whether he intends to sell the stock, and if he thinks it was a conflict of interest."

Jessica was dreading the call as much as I was, but I used her to stay as far away from Maviglio as I could.

My only contribution to the story was a comment from Bill Jones and a quote from the Fair Political Practices Committee, a state agency that decides the punishment for government officials who break rules about financial disclosure. I called Jones first. His secretary patched me through and Jones didn't even wait for a question.

"Hi, Jason. This latest news is extremely troubling. Steve Maviglio should immediately resign as press secretary. He should immediately sell the stock and I am asking that the SEC investigate Mr. Maviglio to determine if he broke any laws."

I didn't need anything else. Jones said it all. This is one reason journalists are not supposed to befriend their sources. If it ever gets to the point to where you have to expose your source for one thing or another, emotions can take over and you hesitate about writing the full story. But I wasn't one to hesitate, not even with Maviglio, whom I hung out with and genuinely liked.

I called the Fair Political Practices Committee office and the spokesman there read me the conflict-of-interest code stating that any state employee who has a financial interest in a company while doing state business with the same company can be heavily fined. And if the SEC investigated Maviglio, he could very well be jailed for insider trading.

I desperately wanted to get this story out on the wire. When Jessica hung up, she let out a huge sigh and said she felt really bad for Maviglio. I did, too. I knew what I was doing was sleazy.

"What did he say?"

"He said he's not selling the stock, that he wasn't involved in the negotiations, and that he has no business dealings with any of the companies he invested in."

"Did he say anything about me?"

"No. He actually was pretty understanding. He said he knew he would have to talk about this sooner or later."

Jessica wrote up her part of the story, and we shared a byline. It took about forty minutes total, between writing and editing, before it went out on the wire. The headline was damning.

GOV'S PRESS SECRETARY BOUGHT ENERGY STOCK WHILE STATE NEGOTIATED POWER CONTRACTS: SEC OF STATE CALLS FOR SEC PROBE

The next day every major newspaper in California had picked up the story and the *Sacramento Bee* and the *Los Angeles Times* wrote their own versions. Jessica and I shared a fifty dollar award from Dow Jones for breaking the story.

By the end of the week, every daily newspaper in California called for Maviglio's resignation.

TWO

I HATE THIN-SKINNED CRYBABY REPORTERS. Journalists are supposed to be tough, like overcooked steak, thick enough to deflect all the harsh criticism. That's what every editor tells you when you start out. But most of the reporters I know can't take a beating, especially if it's from a competitor like me.

Apparently, I gave the competing papers and wire services a good whipping. That's what my editor, Arden Dale, told me in December 2001 when I won Dow Jones Newswires' Journalist of the Year award for a series of stories I broke on California's energy crisis.

When Arden called to tell me about my award, I thought she was going to say, "Jason, we've figured out you're a complete fraud. You're fired." Doesn't she know that I have no idea what I'm doing? Am I that good of an actor?

You could say that I got many scoops through unconventional means. I shared sources with competing reporters on the energy crisis, and those sources would give me the skinny on what my competitors were up to. Then I would run to post my own version on Newswires before it appeared anywhere else. This isn't the usual way reporters get their stories. The usual hack is assigned a beat, and his job is to find out everything that happens on that beat. You're supposed to cultivate sources, whether it's the librarian, janitor, cop, senator, or local grocer… anyone who can feed you information. You can't just sit at your desk and wait for a story to fall into your lap, and you can't rely solely on your sources. You have to do the digging on your own, whether it requires reading the police blotter or the city council agenda. I lucked into the best sources in the business: senators, congressmen, CEOs, stock traders, federal officials. Whenever they got a call from a print or television reporter asking specific questions about the energy crisis, my sources would call me immediately to spill on what was going to be reported. It was the ultimate tip service.

"Jason, it's Richard."

"Hey, buddy. How are you?"

"The *Chronicle* is going to report that Davis wants the state to buy Southern California Edison's transmission lines to keep the company from going bankrupt. You got ninety minutes before the story is posted online."

"Got it. Dinner Friday at Spago?"

"Deal"

All I needed to do was confirm the leak, get a comment from some state official, a stock analyst, and a spokesman at the utility, and then send the story off to be edited. A scoop is a scoop. In my opinion, as long as you are the first one who reports the news, you own the story. It doesn't really matter how you get it. Other journalists will whine about ethics, but that's a load of crap. If reporting a huge story required journalists to pimp their mothers, there would be a lot of elderly hookers on the street.

People ask me how I cultivate sources and get people to talk. It's easy. If I'm talking to a distraught mother, I become her son. If I'm interviewing a CEO, I'll become the loyal employee. I like to think that my own gift is to make people feel comfortable enough to spill anything.

Sources know I'm tenacious and hungry, and get a good high from a good story. My wife Lisa calls it a "vulnerable sweetness" that makes people feel safe around me. She says it's one of the reasons she married me. And it made Lisa, her family, and Maviglio trust me—even when they shouldn't have.

I took a trip to Sacramento in January 2001 to size up the competition and see how much they really knew about the energy crisis and whether I was ever in danger of being scooped. About twice a week, Governor Davis held press conferences at the Capitol building. That's where most of the competing reporters got their "snooze."

In the corridor outside, the pressroom reporters spoke to editors on cell phones and avoided speaking to one another. But everyone knew who was who. Overweight, khaki-wearing print journalists with thin notebooks stuffed into back pockets are easily distinguished from television reporters who wear designer clothing and smell good. Stylistically, I fell somewhere in between the two. I wore designer jeans and expensive button-down shirts. My shoes were "Handmade in Italy" and always polished. I tried to put myself together well, though I'm self-conscious about my weight and when I look in the mirror I don't like what I see. I figured that draping my body in the same clothes male models wore in ads would help. It never did.

Much of what the so-called professionals reported came directly from news releases or press conferences, and most rarely went beyond the pressroom for quotes or information. When journalists asked Gray Davis a serious question like, "Governor, what are you going to do to ensure blackouts don't happen in California this summer?" Davis deflected it and defended his record.

"Before I was governor there were no new power plants built." Davis would say. "Now we have twelve." Blah, blah, blah. The governor reminded me of that guy in the movie *Airplane!* who bores other passengers so much that they commit suicide to avoid another tedious moment.

I knew how much of a threat the competition posed by the quality of the questions they asked. A reporter who asks an in-depth question has a good handle on a story and could scoop you. You never want to ask too many leading questions, otherwise you risk giving away the meat of your story and other reporters would no doubt catch on.

I naively thought that breaking stories on the energy crisis would impress working journalists to look up to me as the new Bob Woodward or Carl Bernstein. But instead of following up on my scoops and going after bad guys, the press corps attacked my credibility. Reporters go out of their way to discredit journalists who continually scoop them. Otherwise they have to explain to their editors why they aren't breaking the same stories. When the press corps rejected me I convinced myself that the whole goddamn world was conspiring against me. All I wanted was to be accepted as a member of their club.

What I found out about my competitors is that most of them are a bunch of lazy fucks who are less inclined to dig for the truth than report bureaucratic bullshit and then go home for the day. They weren't interested in the relentless, gumshoe reporting I shot my wad over. Luckily for me no one in the Sacramento press corps was smart enough to end my writing career by exposing me as the felonious thief and drug addict I was.

Maviglio provoked my paranoid outbursts, telling me that other journalists had me in their gun sights. He told me about taking calls from reporters from the *Sacramento Bee, San Diego Union Tribune*, and *San Francisco Chronicle*, all asking him if there was any truth to a just-posted Newswires story.

"Well, what did you tell them?" I demanded.

"I said I couldn't confirm it." Maviglio said.

"You fucking cocksucker! You know damn well that story is one hundred percent accurate. You fuck."

Maviglio laughed at my outburst. I think he enjoyed pushing my buttons.

"Can you pick me up at LAX Friday?" Maviglio asked.

"Yeah, I guess. What time are you getting in?"

"About 2:00 p.m. Can we stop and get pastrami sandwiches on the way to my hotel?"

"Sure. I hate you. See you Friday."

Ever since my story on him appeared, Maviglio was continually trying to poke holes in my articles to keep reporters from following up on my stories. Maviglio knew that the worst thing he could tell a reporter about someone else's scoop is "no comment." With each "no comment," Maviglio planted a seed in reporters' minds that the story in question could be false. Because I used anonymous sources in my more explosive stories on the energy crisis it became difficult for newspapers like the *Los Angeles Times* and the *San Francisco Chronicle* to verify my claims.

Newspapers have rules about using anonymous sources. Some refuse to use them; others make exceptions depending upon the seriousness of the story. Editors are, by and large, skeptical about anonymous sources. Tipsters usually have an axe to grind. But the only way I was able to glean information about the energy crisis was to quote anonymous sources. Initially I pressed executives at energy companies to go on the record, but they were frightened of being fired or sued by their employers for leaking proprietary information. These same executives told me "off the record" that their companies were breaking market rules to exploit the crisis and boost their company's bottom line.

At a financial newswire, we commonly quoted anonymous sources. Investors trade stocks based on rumors every day. As soon as a story I wrote hit the wire, it would influence the stock price of any number of energy companies I identified in my report. That was a huge ego boost; it meant that people read my stories and trusted the information.

When the Sacramento press corps followed up on my scoops, often they quoted bureaucrats who disputed my reporting. But time and again, the truth eventually proved them all wrong.

For all my preaching about thin-skinned journalists, I must admit that nobody's skin is thinner than mine. Maviglio knew that I would become hostile and insecure every time someone in the press corps picked apart one of my stories. And by promoting distrust of my stories' facts, Maviglio often prevented them from getting bigger play.

In August 2001, I broke a story about Viju Patel, an advisor to Governor Davis who oversaw negotiations on the state's investments in long-term energy contracts, and how he was invested in Allegheny Energy Supply, an energy company with which the state, through Patel, was negotiating a four billion dollar energy contract.

I discovered that Patel sold his shares in Allegheny a few weeks after he helped the state close the books on the four billion dollar contract and before the public knew about the deal. That's insider trading. The SEC rule "Regulation FD" (FD standing for Full Disclosure) means that if you know something about a publicly traded company before the rest of the world, you have to wait to buy or sell your shares, or else you'll go down.

My story identified Patel as the eleventh official whose personal financial interests conflicted with their state job keeping the state plugged in. The dozens of advisers that the governor hired to negotiate power contracts didn't turn in financial disclosure forms, the same form that Maviglio forgot to fill out, when they were hired by the Davis administration in January 2001, shortly after three consecutive days of blackouts rolled through California. When the media found out that some of Davis' energy advisers were also cutting side deals with their brokers, the shit hit the fan. Everyone who worked for the state on energy matters had to sell their energy stocks or quit. Maviglio eventually sold his stock in Calpine and Enron and doing so probably saved his job, although his public excuse was that he unloaded his shares because they were becoming too much of a "distraction."

The scandal forced Davis to fire five of his advisers who bought and sold energy stocks on inside information weeks earlier. It also resulted in Davis taking a beating in the press for two weeks; his blindness to malfeasance inside his administration made the energy crisis even worse. People lost confidence in the governor's ability to stop the crisis from spiraling out of control. His approval ratings tanked so precipitously that the governor's spin doctors came in to manipulate the only situation they could: the news. They started with me.

Patel wasn't a low-level adviser. He was executive manager of the California Department of Water Resources, the state's water agency that was compelled to buy all of California's electricity supplies when the state's two biggest utilities became cash dry.

Patel was a full-time state employee whose job was to oversee all contract negotiations.

After requesting a copy of Patel's financial disclosure form, I immediately spotted a huge story. Patel brokered the deal between the state and Allegheny and was once employed by Allegheny. Between Maviglio's purchase of Calpine and Enron stock during the contract negotiations and now Patel's sale of his Allegheny shares during the same period, there appeared to be a pattern of abuse at the highest level of state government. There was no way I could be ignored once I broke this story—this time I had documents to back it all up.

On August 1, 2001, I called Oscar Hidalgo, spokesman for the Department of Water Resources, for a comment.

"Yo, Oscar. What's up, brother? It's Jason."

I felt bad for the guy because I was about to tell him I was going to break news that would cause other reporters to ring his phone off the hook and force him to stay late at the office to respond to questions about my story.

"Hey bro. How you doin'?"

"Not so good, man. I have bad news. That financial disclosure form you sent me on Patel shows he's got stock in one of the companies you guys signed a contract with…I gotta report this story."

"Dude, you're killing me."

"I know, man. I'm sorry. Can you comment on it?"

"Shit, I don't know anything about this guy. Lemme call Maviglio."

Fuck. I was hoping to avoid Maviglio.

"Okay. Call me back."

I started writing the story using the financial disclosure form as a primary source. I left four messages for Patel at the

Water Resources Department but he never returned my call. It would have been nice to have a comment from him, but the form spoke for itself.

Seconds later, my phone began ringing.

"This is Jason."

"What's up? It's Oscar."

"Hey."

"I can't get any info on Patel. I can give you a general comment."

"That'll work."

"The details of the activities of all the traders who owned stock is still being reviewed. Once completed, it will be released publicly in the next week."

I added that lame-ass comment to my story, sent it off to the copy editors for a quick edit, and waited until it hit the wire. I rubbed my hands together like a mad scientist. At 4:27 p.m. I saw this headline pop up on my computer terminal:

Calif Pwr Mgr Held Stk In Co State Signed $4B Deal With

My work was done for the day. I headed to Al Gelato, an Italian dessert shop that serves some pretty good cannoli. I was meeting Governor Davis' personal assistant, a Korean girl who used the expletive "fuck" to describe every facet of her life, and drank socially like every day was New Year's Eve. She was in Los Angeles visiting her parents. We became fast friends six months earlier because I knew how to make her laugh. Maviglio wanted to date the governor's assistant but she rejected him, so I would tell her jokes about how Maviglio hit on his cat and the cat turned him down. I never pressed her for information about the governor, and I'm sure she had more dirt on him than anyone. But I genuinely liked her as a friend, so I stuck to that and never crossed the line when I hung out with her.

She and I were chatting about Maviglio when my cell phone started to ring. I immediately recognized the number.

"Oh, Mr. Maviglio. What a surprise. I'm sitting here with your woman, making fun of you. Your ears must have been burning."

He totally ignored me and started speaking loudly in a thick New Jersey accent.

"Yo dickhead, you wrote a story that is wrong. Viju Patel doesn't have nothing to do with those long-term contracts. He's in charge of the office supplies. He sets up the chairs and makes sure the copy machine is working. He's a glorified secretary."

"What?"

My body started shaking the same way it did when I was detoxing during my first three weeks in rehab.

"Yeah, asshole," Maviglio said proudly. "Your story is wrong."

"It can't be." I said. My voice showed all of the signs of insecurity and doubt. "His financial disclosure form said he was the executive manager. It said he was in charge of the long-term contracts."

"It's wrong. I'm going to conference in Oscar. Don't go anywhere."

The governor's assistant got a good view of my vulnerable side, which I rarely allowed to come out in public. Maviglio called me back a minute later. I cleared my throat.

"Hel…lo?"

"Yeah. It's Maviglio. I got Oscar on the phone."

Oscar laid into me real good.

"I'm so sick of you reporters and this so-called scandal you're all writing about. Leopold, you didn't do your research. Patel has nothing to do with the long-term contracts. He's in charge of the office equipment. You reporters are trying to make a scandal where none exists. This time you fucked up. You need to fix this. It's my ass on the line. I'm getting calls from every paper in the state trying to follow up on this."

Oh my God, oh my God, oh my God. How could this have happened? I'm fucked. This is going to prove that everyone was right about me. I can't be trusted. I'm a fuck-up. Shit. What do I do?

"Okay. Listen guys. I am sorry. I am really, really sorry. I will retract the story. I promise."

"Good," Maviglio said. "You better call me back. Tell what's-her-name I said hi."

I held the cell phone in my hand just a few inches away from my ear and just stared at the governor's assistant. My eyes were open but I couldn't see her face. I was looking at a police officer who was reading me my Miranda rights as I sat in my principal's office with my parents. I was in the eighth grade. It was exactly one week after my bar mitzvah, when I stole my librarian's credit cards and went on a shopping spree at the Nanuet Mall with my brother, Eric, who just turned sixteen and got his driver's license. Eric used one of the credit cards to buy a leather jacket and I went to Radio Shack to buy a couple of computer games for my TRS-80 color computer. The cashier wouldn't accept the credit card from me unless a parent signed the slip. I told him my mom was in the car, and he said I should go out and get her. I left the store and told my brother, and we peeled out of the parking lot in my mom's station wagon and drove home. The cashier kept the credit card. The next day, while I was sitting in the principal's office, the police officer explained to me that the cashier picked me out of the junior high school yearbook. That was the first time I got arrested. I wound up with a juvenile delinquent record and was expelled from school. When I got home, my father beat the living shit out of me until I saw stars, just like a character in a cartoon does when a safe falls on his head.

I left the governor's assistant at Al Gelato and drove back to my office. Around 6:00 p.m. I called Drew, my editor, at home in New York to tell him what was going on.

"That's bullshit, dude. I don't believe him. If Maviglio is going to claim that Patel is an office manager, then he has to explain why he sold his stock in Allegheny after they negotiated that contract. It doesn't make sense. Think about it. If he's not involved with the contracts, then he shouldn't have to sell that stock. That law only applies to people directly involved in the negotiations."

"Drew, Maviglio has me totally convinced that I'm wrong. I told him if we were wrong we would print a retraction."

"What? You told him that?"

"Yeah"

"Don't do that again until you talk to me first."

"Okay. I'm sorry, dude. I just wanted to get him off the phone and I didn't want him to be mad at me."

"Go back to the office and make some calls and try to find out from someone if they know Patel was involved in the contract negotiations and if they can say that on the record."

I couldn't tell Drew that I promised Oscar and Maviglio that I'd retract the story outright. I knew he'd be pissed at me.

Maviglio and Oscar had made me doubt my reporting. When I got to my desk I opened up my e-mail and saw a message in my inbox—sent out to about fifty reporters in the Sacramento press corps—from Hilary McLean, one of Governor Davis' senior spokespeople. The e-mail immediately transformed my feelings of self-doubt into rage

To: Press Corps
From: Hilary McLean
Re: Dow Jones Story on Viju Patel

The Dow Jones story that ran this afternoon on Viju Patel contains numerous errors and we would like to take this opportunity to set the record straight. Viju Patel did not oversee the state's long-term contract negotiations and he is not involved in the state's energy dealings. He performs the duties of a general office manager. He is in charge of the Xerox machine and orders supplies for the Department of Water Resources. The press office has spoken with Jason Leopold, the reporter who wrote the story on Viju Patel. Jason told Steve Maviglio this evening that he will issue a full retraction stating that his story was wrong.

Hilary McLean
Senior Deputy Press Secretary Governor Gray Davis
Press Office

That bitch. It all makes sense now. Motherfucking unbelievable. She's trying to stop the other papers from picking up my story. That's it. They're trying to discredit me. You don't need to be Woodward or Bernstein to figure out that there's probably some truth—or maybe something bigger—to my story if the press office is going to such great lengths to stop it from being picked up by the *Los Angeles Times*. *Man*, I thought, *if I could only control my drinking and coke habit, I'd pour myself a tall glass of brandy and snort a line or two off my desk.* I don't know how I've been able to stay straight during situations like this.

I signed on to Dow Jones Interactive, the company database that stores nearly every news story and press release written in the world. I searched for Viju Patel and got two hits. The one I wrote a couple of hours earlier and another one from the *San Francisco Chronicle* dated March 18, 2001. As soon as I read the *Chronicle* story and the quote from Patel it became clear that Maviglio, Oscar, Hilary, and probably other Davis cronies in Sacramento had manipulated the shit out of me. This was the headline and quote from Patel that appeared in the *Chronicle* five months before my story.

Davis' Gouging Claims Disputed
Officials Say No Link Between PG&E Bankruptcy, High Prices

"It is a seller's market," said Viju Patel, executive manager of the Department of Water Resources' power systems department. "The power companies do not need an excuse to raise prices."

Patel didn't sound like an office manager tending to the copy machine. I did a Google search for more zingers but nothing came up. Then it hit me. I went on to Governor Davis' website where all of the press releases, transcripts, speeches, and other information are stored. I recalled that Davis held a press conference in February to announce the hiring of experts in the energy industry to handle the negotiations on long-term contracts. That's when Patel was promoted to executive manager at the Department of Water Resources. I went through all the posted press releases to see if the governor made any reference to Viju Patel. Nothing. Then I went onto the Department of Water Resources' website and typed "Viju Patel" into the search engine. Here's what I found:

Viju Patel-Energy Advisor

As technical and policy advisor to the Deputy Director, Mr. Patel analyzes and recommends development of energy policy, legislation, and regulations for CERS. Specific tasks include directing the implementation of DWR policies regarding the acquisition of electric power supply, transmission arrangements, hydroelectric, and other power resources. Responsible for analyzing market and economic conditions, he negotiates and manages energy purchases, sales, and exchanges.

CERS is an acronym for California Energy Resources Scheduling. It's the sub-agency at Department of Water Resources that Davis put in charge of buying all of the state's power. Davis signed an emergency piece of legislation after the blackouts in January 2001, giving CERS carte blanche to spend as much money as it needed to make sure the lights didn't go out again. Patel's bio basically said that he was in charge of the whole damn operation, including oversight of the state's long-term contracts!

I danced around the office and started boxing with my reflection in the window. I started singing the theme song from Rocky III. Then I introduced myself to my imaginary audience.

"Ladies and gentlemen, will you please welcome the undisputed heavyweight champion, JASON LEOPOLD."

I took a deep drag from a cigarette when I called Maviglio to break his balls and demand that he send out an e-mail apologizing to the press corps for discrediting me. I held in the tobacco smoke until Maviglio answered his cell phone. I exhaled loudly as soon as he answered.

"Did you hear that, you asshole? That's the sound of satisfaction."

"Are you running a retraction?"

"No, but you are."

"What do you mean?"

"You know what I'm talking about. Don't fuck with me. Viju Patel isn't an office manager at the DWR."

"Uh, yes he is."

"Uh, no he isn't. I've got the proof, Maviglio. His bio is posted on the DWR website! He's been quoted in the *Chronicle* talking about the state's fucking energy shortage!"

"That's strange. I don't know anything about that. Send me everything you have on Patel and I'll take a look at it," Maviglio said and let out a big yawn.

"No. That's bullshit. You have to send another press release out tonight to the press corps saying you guys made a mistake. You have to clear my name."

"It's ten o'clock! Can't this wait until tomorrow?"

"Maviglio, if it was anyone else you wouldn't be pulling this shit. If I worked at the *Los Angeles Times* my editors would be all over your ass for something like this."

He didn't say a word.

"Hello? Are you there? Do you hear me?"

"Yeah, yeah. Relax. I'll call Hilary and tell her to send out a new press release."

"Speaking of Hilary, I wonder why she said that I would be printing a retraction. I told you that I would print a retraction only if my story was wrong."

"No, you didn't. You said you would go back to the office and run a retraction. Oscar can confirm that."

"You're such a fucking liar."

"I'll call Hilary now."

"I'm not leaving the office until I see that press release. It better go out tonight."

I called Drew at home and woke his wife. She handed the phone to Drew and said, "Guess who?" I told Drew about the press release that Hilary sent out to the press corps discrediting me and how I found Viju's bio on the Department of Water Resources website confirming my story and then some. Drew wasn't able to comprehend what I was saying. It was after one in the morning in New York and he was half asleep.

I sat at my computer clicking the new message button on my inbox for three-and-a-half hours but I didn't get any new e-mails from Hilary or Maviglio. I called Maviglio on his cell phone and went directly into his voicemail. "FUCK YOU!" I hollered into the phone. I did that over and over again until his voicemail was full. Then I called Maviglio's private line in the press office and did the same thing. I didn't know what else to do. It was the only thing I could think of. I drove back to my apartment. It was 2:10 a.m. Lisa was already asleep. I checked my e-mail. Still nothing. I got into bed and stared into darkness. I imagined I was a superhero flying into the capitol building in Sacramento. I borrowed the Lasso of Truth from Wonder Woman and used it to force Maviglio and Hilary to tell the press corps that they lied, my story was accurate, and I was the greatest reporter that ever lived.

I got into the office Thursday morning at 10:00 a.m. and those bastards still hadn't sent out an e-mail to the press corps clearing my name. I called Maviglio before I took my 300 milligrams of antidepressants. That was a mistake.

"Maviglio?"

"Yeah?"

"I'm going to hire someone to chop your cat into little pieces, you piece of shit, you fuck, you asshole, prick, dick, asswipe, fuckface, fucklip, if you don't clear my name now, you pussy."

I sounded like I had Tourette's syndrome. Maviglio hung up on me.

Hilary didn't send out a new press release until 5:00 p.m. on Friday, when all of the other reporters had left for the weekend. The news release was a sentence long. It didn't clear my name or confirm the investigative work I put into my story.

To: Press Corps
From: Steve Maviglio Re: Viju Patel

It has come to our attention that Viju Patel manages the state's energy purchases and ensures that the long-term electricity contracts are signed in a timely manner.

Hilary McLean

Senior Deputy Press Secretary Governor Gray Davis Press Office

This was a strategy Hilary and Maviglio had planned from the minute I broke the story on Patel two days earlier. If you want to ensure that the media don't cover an important political story, send out a press release on a Friday, preferably at the end of the day. By the time reporters return on Monday, the story will be old news and will either be buried deep within a newspaper or not covered at all.

That's what happened with the Viju Patel revelations. No one else ever wrote about him. In fact, only a few people in the press corps got the new press release that Hilary and Maviglio sent out. I heard from other reporters that a majority of the press corps was under the impression that I retracted my story two days earlier, so they never bothered to follow up on it. Only one reporter, columnist Dan Weintraub, who writes about politics for the *Sacramento Bee*, came to my defense. Weintraub also publishes a weekly insider's report on what happens behind the scenes in Sacramento. Only a select few of the movers and shakers in Sacramento get his report; it's only available by e-mail and has nothing to do with the *Bee*. Dan called me after the Patel flap and said he never received a copy of McLean's press release that failed to vindicate me. Weintraub interviewed me, took down my version of the events, and followed up with the governor's office. Dan found out I was right about Patel and wrote in his weekly column that Maviglio and McLean tried to shut down a big story by wrongfully discrediting me.

A week later a columnist from *New Times*, a weekly newspaper in Los Angeles, wrote a story on how the governor's goon squad tried to shut me down. In her column she wrote that I was "one of the most aggressive reporters on the energy crisis." She also quoted a reporter—anonymously—who explained why no one in Sacramento trusted me.

"You can't trust him because he's little more than a business wire version of Matt Drudge."

No one knew how it really went down between me and the press office. And no one knew that I set Maviglio up just a few weeks earlier and nearly cost him his job. What goes around comes around.

THREE

FROM AN EARLY AGE, I had two obsessions: reading newspapers and listening to music. I spent several years interning in the promo departments for a handful of labels, including Warner Bros., Epic, and I.R.S. Records.

When I was twenty years old, skipping classes at NYU and slaving away for I.R.S., I was first introduced to cocaine. I was scared at first when an executive spilled white powder on the solid oak conference table and used a credit card to cut it into what he called "rails." I had never seen cocaine before. Pot and hash were the hardest drugs I had used. I thought back to those propaganda films I was forced to watch in high school, warning about the dangers of drugs. I imagined that the cocaine would rot my teeth, make my nose fall off my face, and turn me into a homeless hustler selling my body to earn enough cash to cop another hit. I guess those images weren't persuasive enough because I was eager to bust my cherry. The executive handed me a rolled-up one-dollar bill and talked me through my first line. I felt like a kid again, learning how to ride a bike for the first time.

"Do you feel that shit dripping down the back of your throat?" the executive asked.

"I think so. It burns." Blood dripped out of my nose, a lot of it. I really was a virgin. I licked the blood off of my hand like the exec told me to, so I wouldn't let coke remnants go to waste.

"Of course it burns. You just put drugs up your nose. How do you feel?"

I felt like I had a hard-on. I felt like those people in Aldous Huxley's *Brave New World* who take Soma to fight depression and make life bearable. Now I could understand why Huxley's characters felt so damn good. Snorting coke for the first time was exactly how I imagined born-again Christians felt when they get baptized and accept Jesus Christ as their savior. Coke for me was a religious experience. I felt an enormous amount of love for the people I usually hated, like my parents and myself. I felt an urge to help the homeless, to give away my money to complete strangers, and to make the world a better place. Just one line erased all feelings of self-doubt.

The coke had me chatting music with the executive for ten hours straight. We called our families to say hello. We called friends we hadn't spoken to in years. We called ex-girlfriends to see if they wanted to get back together.

The coke kept me awake until the middle of the following afternoon. I crashed hard. I popped two Xanax, and slept until the next morning. By the time I woke I felt overwhelmed with guilt, just like the characters in *Brave New World* when they didn't take their Soma. I needed more coke to wipe away the guilt.

The executive at I.R.S. told me about a bar on Thirteenth Street where I could buy a small bag of coke for forty dollars.

Sitting at the end of the bar was an older black man in a ragged army jacket and trucker hat. He seemed out of place. The other patrons looked like long-haired wannabe rockers. Tunes like Aerosmith's "Dream On" blared from the jukebox at full volume. Every few minutes some dude would walk up the black guy and give him a soul shake. A couple minutes later, he returned the gesture. I figured he was the guy I was looking for. I walked toward him like an old friend who hadn't seen him in years.

"What's up, man? Long time no see," I said.

"How you been?" he replied, like he knew me. Palming two twenty-dollar bills, I shook the black man's hand. His skin felt like rough leather. He peeked at the money, put his hand inside his pants pocket, and handed a small package to me underneath the bar counter.

I held that package tight, making a beeline to the unisex piss-drenched bathroom. Roaches were crawling up the walls on top of local band flyers. I sat on the toilet and looked with love at the mini-Ziploc bag. It was beautiful. Two rocks. I took my NYU identification card from my wallet, held the bag of coke up against the wall, and feeling like a pro I pressed my NYU ID card against the bag, crushing the rocks until they turned into powder. I inserted a tightly-rolled dollar bill into the bag and snuffled like a pig. The effects were immediate.

It took about three months to become addicted to coke. At first, it was only weekend use. But soon enough I was snorting it, a lot of it, every day. I needed to stay high because I couldn't stand the comedowns. I stopped going to my classes at NYU. Then I stopped going to I.R.S. to fulfill the obligations of my internship. I stopped calling my friends and family and even forgot to ask my parents to pay my tuition.

I lost about thirty-five pounds because I no longer felt like eating when coked up. I slept in my clothes and didn't take off my boots for weeks at a time. When I finally did remove the Doc Martens, I found a thick black tar growing between my toes. When I was high, I would pull out chunks of long hair from the back of my head. One day, I caught a glimpse of myself in the mirror and saw that one side of the long hair on the back of my head was a couple of inches shorter than the other side. It looked like I had half a mullet.

I sold everything I owned to buy coke. I took my CD collection to a second-hand record store and hocked it. I stole my roommate's stereo, VCR, and jewelry, and pawned it. I sold his college textbooks back to NYU for cash. I broke into the apartment of a stripper friend and robbed her of about 200 one-dollar bills people had stuffed into her G-string.

When I ran out of money and there was nothing left to sell or steal, I went to the bar and asked the dealer to spot me four bags of coke. He refused.

"Bro, I'm your best customer. Come on!"

"Look at you, man. You fucking an addict. I don't give credit to no addict," he said in broken English.

"What are you talking about? I ain't no addict. I'm not asking you to spot me for me. It's for a record company exec who's in town. He asked me to hook him up," I weaseled.

"Yeah? Why he no come with you here?" the black man asked me.

"'Cause he's well-known. You know, he doesn't want to be recognized."

"Well, okay man. I give you four. But you be here 6:00 p.m. tomorrow and pay me. You not here then, I deal with you in not-so-friendly way."

He gave me the four bags and I hightailed it out of there and got back to my dorm room as fast as possible. When I got to my building, I found that NYUs housing manager had left an envelope for me marked: "Urgent."

Dear Mr. Leopold:

Your repeated failure to pay your New York University Housing bill leaves us no alternative but to demand that you vacate your living quarters by Sunday. The locks will be changed first thing Monday morning and your NYU Identification Card will be suspended. You will not be authorized to enter Carlyle Court until the $7,351 balance is paid.

Sincerely,
NYU Housing

I tore up the letter and threw it in the trash. I didn't give a shit. I had already failed all of my courses. I went to my room, locked myself in the bathroom, poured out a bag of coke on the toilet seat lid and cut myself two huge fat lines, one for each nostril. I stared at my reflection in the mirror. I was finally staring at the truth. I was a drug addict.

No matter how much coke I put up my nose, I couldn't OD. I swallowed thorazine to help me fall asleep.

The moment I ran out of coke I was consumed with guilt. I laid myself down in bed, wrapped a telephone cord around my neck, and tried to hang myself—lying down. If there was a How To Commit Suicide Hotline, I would have called it. I hated myself. I just wanted to die.

It was Sunday afternoon, and NYU's housing manager broke in my room to escort me out of the building. I must have looked ragged. My jeans were two sizes too big and I didn't have a belt to hold them up. I hadn't taken a shower for over a month. Still, the housing manager didn't comment on my appearance.

"Please," he said. "Hurry up and leave."

When I got downstairs, the security guard said there were two black men who stopped by to see me.

"They looked pretty shady," the security guard said. "I refused to let them upstairs. They told me to tell you that you need to contact them immediately about a business transaction."

"Okay. Thanks."

All I had left was a subway token, eighty-three cents in my pocket, and a knapsack on my back. I took the A train to Washington Heights, got out and walked across the George Washington Bridge to New Jersey. At the border, where New York and New Jersey meet, I stopped to look over the guardrail into the Hudson River. It was black. Pitch black. I couldn't see the water. It was just nothingness, like when you close your eyes just before you fall asleep. I stared at the blackness. My heart started to beat faster when my thoughts turned to jumping. I picked up a rock and dropped it over the railing. But I was too scared to die, even though I felt it was my only way out. I continued walking. When I got into Fort Lee, just a few hundred yards past the end of the George Washington Bridge, I walked to a bus station and sat down on the bench.

I was hungry. I hadn't eaten in three days. I was still strung out on the last of the coke and still a bit groggy from the thorazine I took the night before last. I grabbed my knapsack and walked into the A&P supermarket just above the bus station. I had no idea what I could buy with eighty-three cents.

"Kidney beans!"

I grabbed a can of Progresso beans. A produce clerk was nice enough to open the can of beans for me. I paid for the food—had enough change left over for one phone call—and went back to the bus depot outside. I felt like a bum eating beans out of the can. It was 12:45 in the morning, and I had two things on my mind: how I was going to get home and how I was going to kill myself.

On my trip across the bridge, I picked up an empty beer bottle and put it in my knapsack. When I got to the other side I sat down on a bus bench and took the bottle out and repeatedly hit myself in the head, hoping to knock myself unconscious. It didn't work. I just became dizzy and lumpy.

The longest two hours of my life passed. Tired and cold, I couldn't sit still. Then it started to rain. I smashed the bottle on the cement and picked up a chunk of glass. Slowly, I started to slice my forehead. Drops of blood fell onto my lips and my white T-shirt. I couldn't tell whether my face was wet from the rain or the blood. The scheme was to appear like I had just been mugged. Every half-hour a police cruiser drove by, but none stopped. No free ticket to the hospital.

"Please, God, help me get out of here," I prayed, looking up toward the sky.

Two minutes later a red Toyota MR2 stopped beside me. Was this the devil in disguise? The driver shouted through the side window:

"Hey! You need a ride?"

"Yeah. Rockland County."

"Get in. I'm headed in that direction."

When I got into the car the driver told me it would cost ten dollars for the ride home.

"I have some change. That's it."

"Pay me when you get home."

The driver said he was on a mission to score cocaine and was driving people around all night for cash. He needed twenty dollars more for a gram. Ignoring the blood on my face, he drove a vacant Palisades Parkway. The rain obstructed our view of the pavement; it was so black outside it looked like we were driving into hell. The driver was moving his jaws, but I was oblivious to everything he said. He kept shooting me looks, and for a moment or two I thought he was going to try and rape me. He stomped on the gas pedal and my head jerked back as the car slid out of control across the lanes. I hoped that the car would flip and kill me instantly, but the driver gained control once again.

"Whoa," he marveled. "That was close."

As we gained on my Rockland County exit, I started to get anxious about the ten bucks I didn't have.

He exited the Palisades Parkway and I directed him toward my folks' house with its four tin Roman columns. Pure suburbia.

As the driver pulled into the driveway, I flung open the door and started to run. I didn't stop. I just kept running, into the woods. Running. That's what I did best.

Through the trees, I heard the driver yell, "Jason! Jason!" but I kept running until his voice fell to a whisper and finally was completely out of range.

I fell to the dirt, curled up into a fetal position and let the rain pour over me. I wanted to fade away into the darkness.

I lay there in the mud until seven in the morning. That's when my father left for work and I knew it would be safe to go into the house. When the sun rose, I looked down at my clothes. My T-shirt had blood and dirt stains. My jeans were torn at the knees and my sneakers were caked with mud. I stood up and walked out of the woods, which led to the backyard of my house. Suddenly I noticed that my folks' house was white.

It had been six months since I had been home. During that time, I had managed to turn into a full-blown drug addict and thief. Why didn't I just tell my parents something was drastically wrong with me and the way I was raised? My father used to excuse all his fuck-ups by saying there weren't any books written on how to be a parent. And I believed him until I got a job in a bookstore and noticed that a couple of shelves were filled with how-to books on raising children. Duped again.

There weren't any cars in the driveway. My mother would be home, though. She was supposed to be at work at 9:00 a.m., but it took her hours to put on makeup, do her hair, drink a pot of coffee, smoke cigarettes, and watch some television. She usually got to the office at around 2:00 p.m. and left at 5:00 p.m. She lied to her boss, telling him she was out at meetings. The next day she would repeat the same routine.

"Here's the plan," I told myself. "Go inside the house, pack, pretend you're moving out. Mom will start to cry and you'll probably argue with her and she'll wanna know what happened to you the past six months. Don't tell her anything. Lie. And don't forget to kill yourself before your father gets home."

I walked up to the front door. My key didn't fit. The locks were changed. I knocked. My older brother, Eric, opened the door a crack. I tried to push my way in but he used his foot as a doorstop.

"You're not allowed in," he said.

"Why not?"

"Because."

"Because why?"

"Because nobody wants you here. Now leave."

"No. Let me in."

"Leave or I'll call the police."

"You're a fucking asshole."

He slammed the door. Bastard. Five months ago, Eric visited me at NYU and we celebrated his twenty-seventh birthday. I took him out around the city. Then Eric, some of my friends, and I went back to my dorm room to party. When I broke out the coke, he didn't hesitate. He snorted lines with me. I thought we bonded.

I walked around the corner where my sister, Michelle, and her boyfriend pulled up in a beat-up pickup truck. She got out of the car, ran over to me, and started crying. I always had a good relationship with her, but she was so naive. She didn't understand why I hated myself so much. Her life was simple: boyfriend, job, friends.

"Jason, are you on drugs?" she asked me, sobbing.

I couldn't help it. Tears poured out of my eyes. "No. Just go home," I said. "I'm not on drugs."

"You look anorexic," she said.

She put her arms around me and I felt her tears fall onto my neck. Her hug was the single greatest emotional experience I ever shared with a member of my family.

When a police car pulled up she got back into her boyfriend's pickup truck and they drove away. A second cop car pulled up, sirens blaring. Then came two more cop cars, and then another. I was surrounded. Neighbors stared through curtains and screen doors. Some were brave enough to stand on their front porches.

"Son, you have to leave. Your family does not want you around," one of the police officers said to me.

"I don't have anywhere to go," I said.

"Are you abusing drugs?" the cop asked me.

"No."

"What happened to your clothes? Why do you have blood on your shirt?"

"I don't know."

"Your parents told us you live in the city. I suggest you go back there. You can catch a bus from the shopping center. We'll drive you."

The police dropped me off at the shopping center, near the bus stop. I walked over to a pay phone and called my mother. When she picked up the phone I started to curse at her and threatened to jump off the Tappan Zee Bridge. That's how I wound up in that mental institution in the summer of 1993. My father was listening in on the other line. He called the police again and told them to take me away. The same six cops pulled up next to me at the shopping center.

"We had a feeling we'd be back," one of the cops said.

They put me in handcuffs and drove me to the Pomona Mental Health Center. The cops said my parents had called the police because a man in their driveway was shouting my name and knocking on their door demanding ten dollars. The police arrested the guy. They said they and my parents knew I was abusing drugs.

My father worked fifteen blocks from my dorm room. I wondered why he didn't he try to help me.

FOUR

FTER BEING RELEASED FROM the mental hospital, I was clean, but I was also unemployed.

I missed the glamorous life, the music biz. I got a job at a newspaper writing obituaries, but it was depressing. I often felt like crying after calling the family of the deceased.

"Oh, Jesus, I can't believe he's really gone," the widow would sob to me when I asked questions like, "What was the first thing your husband did when he got home from work?"

"He came into the kitchen...and he...Why, God? Why? What will I do now? What will I do?"

Calls like this seriously made me want to hang myself. I couldn't deal with the pain.

I tried to score a job at a record company. I asked a former contact if he had anything available. "You're shit out of luck. There aren't any openings I know of."

I cold-called the promotion and publicity departments of every major and independent record label. Twenty-four rejections later, I finally hit pay dirt when I got the head of publicity at Milan Entertainment who told me she needed help generating publicity for soundtracks. She told me to send over my resume.

The publicity director and the label's CEO hired me on the spot when I showed them I was familiar with every soundtrack the company had released. In February 1995, they gave me a part-time position that paid 250 dollars a week.

Soon I started hanging out at a bar called the Pit Stop, on Thirteenth Street and Third Avenue. Pit Stop was a block away from a friend's apartment where I was staying. I went to the bar every day.

I befriended the Pit Stop's bartender and owner, Maury, an overweight thirty-something Jewish guy from Long Island who sounded vaguely Italian and walked like a penguin. The Pit Stop had a fake New York license plate behind the bar that said "MAFIA."

I told Maury I worked for a record company and could get him some CDs for the bar's jukebox. I also told him that if he ever needed concert tickets he should talk to me, that I had friends at other record labels and could hook him up.

"That's very nice of you," Maury said. "I woood be very happy if youse coood help me out a lil bit. Then, maybe I woood do sumthin fo you," he said.

"I would be happy to," I said. "It wouldn't cost me anything. We have tons of promotional copies."

Maury and I talked about heavy metal music for about an hour. Then, out of nowhere, he popped the question that literally gave me goosebumps.

"Hey. Doo you party?" Maury asked me.

"What do you mean?" I asked.

"Whadda ya mean wha do I mean? You know," he said tapping his nostril. "Do yoo party?"

Fuck. It had been months since I did blow. Instead of thinking what the drug turned me into, I started to think about how I felt when I snorted my first line. I could handle it this time around. The rationalizations were strange and torturous.

Now that I knew coke could turn me into a fiend, I could control my appetite for the drug and not allow myself to get out of control. I wanted Maury to know that I was cool. I wanted to show off and tell people that I know someone who owns a bar. I imagined walking into the Pit Stop with some friends and everyone saying "Jason!" I would be so popular.

"Yeah," I said. "I party."

Maury invited me into the bathroom and gave me a toot. He told me to make a fist and he poured a little coke onto my palm. It was like being reacquainted with a long-lost love. I was hooked again. I started buying coke from Maury right away. My paycheck from Milan was too small to support my recreational drug use, so I figured out a way to buy the stuff.

Every record company sends promotional records to radio stations, magazines, newspapers, and record stores; hundreds of promos are also stocked in the record company office. The only difference between a promo and regular CD is that the barcode on the promo has a hole punched through it so that it can't be resold at a chain like Tower Records or Best Buy. Most mom-and-pop record stores sell thousands of promo copies at discount—many of which are sold to them by industry hacks.

I grabbed ten CDs, all soundtracks to Hollywood movies, from a metal storage cabinet in the supply room before I left Milan's offices for the evening. Then I took the N train to West 4th Street and headed to a record store on Bleecker Street to sell the CDs. The buyer gave forty-five dollars for the bunch. I used the money to buy coke at the Pit Stop. It was a revelation, like getting drugs for free. I figured it was just a job perk. My father had "fringe benefits," too. He used to bring home toilet paper and paper towels from his office to save on grocery shopping. Dad was cheap that way. After wiping my ass with the cheap sandpaper-like TP, I began to long for the top-dollar brand variety.

Some of New York City's seediest characters, including members of the Hell's Angels, called the Pit Stop home. You could hear the Angels coming from ten blocks away. They traveled in packs, on custom-built Harley Davidson motorcycles with huge, chrome exhaust pipes and bright, metallic painted gas tanks.

Maury waited for the Angels on the sidewalk outside and set out orange cones to secure their parking spaces in front of the bar. The Angels backed up their bikes and lined them up perfectly. The Angels were from central casting—cigarettes, tattoos, and their denim jackets were embroidered with "Hell's Angels New York MC" in gothic lettering.

The Angels could be as loud as they wanted, make a mess, hit on the female bartenders, and kick you off of your barstool if they wanted to sit there. Like a rebellious schoolgirl, I fell for the Angels. I wanted to be part of their clique. I wanted people to fear and worship me, too. I knew I couldn't be a member of their club—I didn't even have a motorcycle—but I asked Maury if it would be possible to be introduced to them.

"Yeah, I guess so," he said.

"Esscuse me fellas," Maury said to the Angels. "I wanna introduce you to a new friend of mine. This is Jason. He works in the music biz. He's a good guy. He got me CDs for the jukebox."

"Hey. It's great to meet all of you. Listen, if you ever need anything, CDs, concert tickets, whatever, let me know and I'll get it for you," I said, trying to buy my way into their inner circle. "Can I buy you guys a round of drinks?"

A few of the Angels shook my hand, but they never disclosed their names. They barely paid me any attention. I was just one more civilian trying to kiss their asses. I gave the bartender a fifty-dollar bill and told her to use it to pay for the Angels' alcohol.

I felt a hand on my shoulder as I turned to walk away.

"Hey you, appreciate the drink. I'm Johnny."

Johnny Hollywood was in charge of entertainment for the Hells Angels. I don't know what that entailed; I felt too stupid to ask him what it meant. He earned his name after appearing as a biker in dozens of movies. He even had an agent. Johnny always wore sunglasses, a bandanna around his forehead, and the de rigueur fringed leather jacket underneath the denim jacket that identified him as a Hell's Angel.

"Nice to meet you," I said. "I'm Jason. Hope I'm not being out of line here," I said, voice cracking a bit. "Would you like to partake in a little tutelage?"

"What, you mean blow? Lead the way."

Johnny followed me into a bathroom stall and locked the door. We were uncomfortably close. I took out the mini-Ziploc from my jeans' coin pocket. It was filled with coke. I handed it to Johnny. He had his own straw. He dipped it into the bag and nearly snorted all of the powder like a human vacuum cleaner.

"Goddamn that's some good shit," Johnny shouted as he punched the wall and scared the shit out of me. "Woo-hoo!"

Johnny mussed my hair and shook my hand, soul-style. Guess I was in.

I didn't do any real work my first year at Milan. I spent most of the time coming up with excuses about why it was difficult to generate media coverage for the soundtracks they released that year.

"It takes time to cultivate relationships with people in the media," I told the CEO. "Music writers rarely review soundtracks. Give me time. I'll make it happen. You gotta trust me."

I was lost. I thought the job would boost my self-esteem, but it didn't. I didn't know what I was doing with my life. I hated being stuck inside of my own skin. I didn't care about anything or anyone. I didn't know how to ask for help and I don't think I wanted any. If I had feelings, I wanted to anesthetize them. I developed a reputation within the music industry for being a lush, but everyone I hung out with thought that was cool. I was always the life of the party and made everyone laugh. My fair-weather friends adored me because, even though I couldn't help myself, I helped them. I always got late-night phone calls from friends who needed advice about careers, girlfriends, boyfriends, and dealing with dysfunctional families. I was a sympathetic ear, a good listener. I created a character—one who has all of the qualities of a child (think Tom Hanks in the movie *Big*), and assumed that role whenever I was in the company of other people.

Every night I partied with record industry hacks and got piss drunk. Then I would sneak over to the Pit Stop and buy coke and hang out until four or five in the morning. My friends who worked in the music industry weren't into cocaine and didn't even know I was using. Drinking made me crave cocaine. My friends always called me the next day to find out what happened to me.

"Oh man," I said. "I was so fucked up. I don't even remember."

"Leopold, you are insane!" my friends said, impressed with my excess. "You must have a nasty hangover, you sick motherfucker."

"Nah. I'm a fucking machine."

Sniffing coke had one positive attribute: it killed any chance of me getting a hangover because once I started doing cocaine I stopped drinking alcohol. I usually slept only two hours—from seven to nine in the morning—and then I woke up and went to work where I would take ten- to twenty-minute catnaps inside the bathroom stall a few times a day.

Ironically, after the head of publicity left Milan, I was promoted and chosen to fill her shoes. I went to celebrate at the Pit Stop where Maury cut a huge piece of coke off of the baseball-sized rock from the safe in his apartment upstairs. He put my portion on a scale. It weighed about three grams. He charged me 120 dollars, eighty dollars cheaper than what I would have paid another dealer.

"Yo, I wanna indroduce you to some guys. They wanna talk to you 'bout a business idea," Maury said, using the tip of a knife to scoop up the excess cocaine off the scale. "That cool witch you?"

"Yeah," I said, snorting a fat line of coke off the top of his portable refrigerator. "Who are they?"

"Lenny and Bruno. They're real close friends o' mine. Dey wanna talk to you."

Lenny and Bruno were sitting at a table near the rear exit of the Pit Stop. They both wore shorts, tennis shoes, and Hawaiian shirts. Lenny had a Mohawk and had a massive build, like the Incredible Hulk. Nothing but solid flesh. He must have weighed 350 pounds.

Bruno looked awfully small next to Lenny, but he would have been called a fat piece of shit if he were sitting there on his own. The buttons on his shirt looked like they were going to pop off at any moment.

"Maury's been tellin' me for munts bout dis great guy who gives him CDs," Lenny said, in a thick Brooklyn accent that sounded like Robert De Niro straight out of *Goodfellas*. Bruno shook his head in agreement. "I says Maury whose dis guy? Is he blowin' you? I gotta meet him. And here you are."

"Well, that's very nice…umm…thank you…Maury…nice compliment," I said, sounding extremely shy and nervous. I started to bite my cuticles, a habit I picked up when I was a kid. When I get nervous I tear the skin off of my fingers with my teeth until they bleed.

"Maury says you're big time in da rekkid biz," Lenny says.

"Well, I wouldn't say big time. I mean, I just got promoted to director of media relations today. So I'm gettin' up there."

"Look at dis," Lenny said to Bruno. "Dis guy's a fucking director. Sounds pretty fucking big to me. As such, I wanted to meet with you and discuss a proposition."

"Yes?"

"I assume you know other rekkid types like you right?"

"Of course. I even hang out with DJs from radio stations. Sometimes we meet the bands, too."

"You friends wit dese people? You go out wit dem?"

"Mmm hmm."

"Good. I want you to start asking dese people if dey wanna buy coke from you. I want you to be my dealer in da entatainment industry"

I should have turned down Lenny's offer right away. But I didn't want to. I wanted the job. I wanted to wear the black hat.

"That sounds like a great idea," I told Lenny. "I would love to do this for you."

"Yeah? Look at dis fucking guy," Lenny said to Bruno and Maury while patting me on the back. "He's got balls like a fuckin' horse."

Lenny reached into a duffel bag underneath the table and took out a paper bag that was rolled up like a burrito. He stuffed the bag down my pants.

"Dat's two grand in coke," Lenny said. "You unload it all I'll give you 750. I'll be back in two weeks for the cash and whateva coke is left over. Anyone fucks witch choo beep me, and me and Bruno will take care of it. Here's my beeper number"

"Deal."

"Awright. Come ere."

Lenny hugged me. There was so much of him.

Bruno shook my hand and put his other arm around my shoulder, confiding to me, "Lenny, he likes you. I can tell. Dat's big. Means sumthin."

Lenny and Bruno then got into a cream-colored Cadillac El Dorado and sped away.

The first rule of dealing drugs is to not be addicted to the stuff you're supposed to sell. I sampled the merchandise as soon as Lenny and Bruno were gone. The coke was pre-packaged into fifty tiny Ziploc bags. I snorted one of them. It tasted horrible. It was cut with too much baby powder. But it still got me high.

I didn't sell any of the coke during those two weeks. I'd dip into the stash, take out a bag and say, "Just this once," or "I'll replace it tomorrow," or "This is the last time I'm gonna do coke on a Thursday." I couldn't control myself. I had all this coke at my disposal and the urge to use it was overpowering.

I sniffed most of the coke myself and ran out of the cash one day before I was supposed to meet Lenny and pay him his two grand. I used my entire paycheck from Milan during those two weeks to pay for drinks, dinners, and cab rides. I panicked. I started picturing myself as one of those deadbeats in Mafia movies that winds up getting dumped in a shallow grave. How the hell was I going to get two thousand bucks in twenty-four hours?

I went back to my apartment and grabbed an old cream-colored leather suitcase that had been in my family for decades and took a cab to Milan's office. It must have been around 1:30

in the morning. I signed in at the security desk. The guard knew me.

"Working late tonight, Jason, huh?" he said.

"Yeah, got a lot of work I need to do before the weekend," I said. Paranoid as hell, I kept looking down at my shoes while the guard spoke to me.

"Getting out of town?" he asked, pointing to my suitcase.

"I'm not sure yet," I said as I walked toward the security gate. "Maybe a last-minute trip. I gotta get some stuff from my office."

I walked directly to the metal storage locker where we keep the promotional CDs. I emptied out half the locker, about 450 CDs, and packed them into my suitcase. My heart was pounding like crazy. I went into my office and poured some coke onto my desk. I used my employee ID to cut it into a line, and snorted it. I used my palm to wipe away the white powder embedded in the desk's wooden grooves and licked it off my hand.

Packed with all the CDs, the suitcase seemed to weigh 200 pounds. It took all my strength to drag it to the elevator. Exiting the ground floor, I lugged the monster bag across the marble tiled floor. I couldn't help but look directly at the security guard, quite sure that he was going to start interrogating me, but he didn't. He opened the front door, hailed a cab, and helped me lunge the suitcase into the trunk of the taxi. Then he pulled a Kleenex out of his inside pocket.

"Here," he said, "your nose is running."

I called in sick the next morning and spent most of the day unloading the CDs at indie record stores on Bleecker Street. I made 2,200 dollars. I told the manager of the last record store I went to that he could keep the suitcase.

I had about an hour to kill before I had to meet Lenny at the Pit Stop, so I spent fifty dollars on sushi. Lenny wanted to meet me in Maury's apartment, a few flights up from the Pit Stop. I went into the bar first and ordered a tall glass of Jack Daniels. No ice. I gave the bartender a twenty and told her to keep the change. Maury and I snorted a few lines while we waited for Lenny, who was already thirty minutes late. I was just about to snort another line when someone started banging on Maury's door.

"It's them," he said.

Maury kissed Lenny and Bruno on the cheek. I stood up also and was just about to pucker my lips, but Lenny said, "Siddown."

"You got my money?" he asked.

"Yup," I said, handing Lenny twenty hundred-dollar bills, "Two Gs. It's all there."

"I hear you been givin away my stuff," he said. "You ain't been sellin any of it like I told you."

"Who said that? I got your money," I said.

"Ay!" Lenny said, "You talkin' back to me? Bruno, did this scumbag just talk back to me? I asked you a question, shithead. You been givin' away my stuff?"

My legs started to shake. I felt like I was about to pee in my pants.

"Yes. I haven't been charging people for using the coke," I admitted.

"Where'd you get da cash?" Lenny asked.

"I took CDs from my office and sold them to get the money."

"Wait a minute, hold on a sec, wait a minute, whadidja do?"

Lenny seemed very intrigued by my scam. I explained how record stores pay cash for CDs and how I stole them from my office and sold them to get his two grand.

"You got access to dese rekkids?" he asked.

"Yup"

"What? Hundreds, thousands?"

The questions Lenny asked me made me feel like a genius. He was no longer speaking to me like I was a lowlife. The tone of his voice sounded like he was giving me some respect.

"Thousands. I order them all the time. We keep about four or five hundred in the office, but the warehouse in Indiana is where everything else is kept."

"No shit."

"Mmm hmm. CDs are like cash. It's kinda like I have access to a bank. Whenever I need cash I just grab some CDs to sell."

Lenny looked at Bruno. They both shook their heads, like they knew what the other was thinking.

"I want a piece," Lenny said. "You're gonna start doing dat for me. Selling CDs. Givin me cash. That'll be the way you make it up to me for not selling the coke."

Lenny pulled out a syringe from his coat pocket. He flicked it and pulled back the plunger. He put the needle on his bicep and injected himself.

"You're gonna do this or you're gonna get a bullet in the head," Lenny said to me. He looked directly into my eyes when he spoke to me, like he was totally oblivious to the needle in his arm. He kept talking and pushed the plunger on the syringe further down until the liquid disappeared. I watched him, my mouth gaping wide at the sight of him shooting himself with steroids as he threatened to kill me.

"You hear me? A bullet in the head," Lenny said, tapping his head with his index finger.

Lenny said he wanted me to deliver fifteen hundred dollars to him from the CDs I sold at the end of the month. He said he would give me one hundred dollars for expenses and cocaine so

I wouldn't slack off on the job. I didn't dare argue. I felt defeated. I figured if things got out of hand I would just kill myself.

I went back to my apartment. I had one new phone message.

"Jason, it's John at the office," said the voice on the answering machine, "Give me a call. We were robbed last night. Someone emptied out the CD closet."

FUCK!

I was paranoid. *John is trying to tell me that he knows I stole the CDs*, I thought. But the sound of his voice on my machine sounded like he was trying to tell me something. I played back the message again.

Yeah, he knows something. He's not just filling me in on the drama; he wants to see what my reaction will be. I called John at the office.

"Hey, John," I said, trying to make my voice sound hoarse so John would believe I was really sick, the reason I gave for staying home from work. "Got your message. What the fuck is going on?"

"Yeah, dude. Someone ripped us off," he said.

"Well, that's weird, 'cause I was in the building last night with some radio station DJS. I took 'em up to see the office and loaded 'em up with CDs. It didn't look like anything was missing when we left."

"Dude, we're missing around six or seven hundred CDs. Did you give those guys that many?"

Shit, I knew we weren't missing that many CDs. John miscounted. I only took 450. How the fuck am I gonna tell John he's wrong without incriminating myself?

"No, John," I said, becoming defensive, "I didn't give away 700 CDs. Are you sure that many are missing?"

"Who cares how many are missing. We're missing a lot. I just stocked the cabinet last week. Now everything's gone."

"Like I said, everything was there when I left last night. It's weird. Maybe the cleaning crew took 'em."

"Security is checking."

John said he was going to let the CEO know that I was in the office last night and gave some CDs away. He hung up the phone. I snorted some coke and put the incident out of my mind. Thinking about it made me paranoid. I was relieved the weekend was here. When I went back to work on Monday the inquiry into the missing CDs was over and done with.

I came up with a simple plan for looting Milan's warehouse in Indiana. First, I told everyone at the office I was launching a promotional campaign with a bunch of AM and public radio stations to help build awareness for the label. To do so, I said, I would be sending the radio stations some CDs to give away every time a DJ played a track from one of Milan's soundtracks. I told everyone it was free publicity. The DJs would say "Milan Entertainment" every time they gave the CD away, and people would soon know that Milan is in the soundtrack business. My colleagues loved the idea.

However, instead of sending the CDs to the radio stations, I had them shipped directly to a record store on Bleecker Street and used some phony radio station call letters in place of the name of the record store. I went the extra mile in covering my tracks for this con. To get the warehouse in Indiana to fulfill orders for promo CDs, I needed to fill out a form and have it signed by a supervisor. So I got an old form that John had filled out, and I pasted his signature onto the bottom of a new form, and faxed it to Indiana.

I spoke with the owner of the record store on Bleecker Street before I hatched the plan, and we struck a deal where I would ship him about 100 CDs every week, which he would then resell to some people he knew in Europe. I collected 2,000 dollars from the guy at the record store at the end of the month, gave Lenny his 1,500 dollars (without his knowing that I put 500 dollars in my pocket), and got a huge bag of free coke and one hundred dollars from him to cover my expenses.

This went on for seven months. I sold thousands of CDs and gave Lenny a bucketful of money during that time. My coke habit got progressively worse, and the drug made me so paranoid that I thought my own shadow was another person stalking me. Not only was I using the coke Lenny gave me, but I also bought my own supply with the extra money I got from the monthly CD sales.

The more I stole from the record label the shittier I felt as a human being. But the guilt didn't stop me from stealing. I don't know why Milan didn't fire me. I must have been a skilled con man, I guess. I spent those seven months writing phony weekly reports and bullshitting the CEO and the rest of the staff about the work I did for the label. The label folk kept praising me. I wanted to get out and start fresh all over again, but I buried myself in shit. I couldn't get out. Then, like a gift from God, I met Lisa Brown.

It was meant to be. God, an angel, an alien, whoever or whatever, put Lisa in my life at the exact moment before the last remaining piece of my world blew away, and said, "Here. You have a choice. You can call this woman and save your life or you can keep doing what you're doing and die."

I met Lisa Brown in March of 1996 in Los Angeles, at a studio screening of the independent movie *Manny & Lo*. Lisa worked for a woman who picked songs for movies, a music supervisor.

I was at the *Manny & Lo* screening with Milan's chief executive, seeing whether or not we wanted to release the soundtrack. We were also in Los Angeles to attend the Grammy Awards and all of its vacuous parties.

Hell-bent on living the life of a rock star, I drank a half bottle of straight whiskey and snorted eight balls of cocaine nearly every day. I had longish hair, pierced ears, and a tattoo on each of my biceps. I wore tight black jeans, a T-shirt flaunting the name of the latest heavy metal band, a leather biker jacket, a studded belt, and motorcycle boots. Unfortunately, I couldn't afford a motorcycle.

When I first met Lisa at the screening, she handed me a business card. It wasn't hers; it was the director's. Milan passed on the movie soundtrack to *Manny & Lo*, but when I got back to New York I tracked Lisa down and phoned her. For anyone who thinks there's no such thing as fate, I offer this up as evidence that it really does exist.

I couldn't recall what Lisa looked like. I don't even know why I bothered to call her. I think I uttered a total of three words to her at the screening: hello, thank you, bye. I wasn't thinking about her romantically. I just picked up the phone in my office at the record company one day and dialed Lisa's phone number. That simple twist of fate saved my life—literally—and would turn out to be the smartest thing I ever did.

"May I speak with Lisa Brown? This is Jason Leopold at Milan Entertainment calling," I said.

"Hi, Jason Leopold. This is Lisa Brown." Lisa had the perfect female voice. It was the kind of voice that could make you fall in love instantly. It was sexy, a wee-bit raspy, and innocent. It was a voice that could comfort you when you're depressed and turn you on to get you in the mood. I couldn't imagine her voice in a scream or showing signs of anger or cursing. Speaking to her was like having phone sex, except that Lisa didn't need to talk dirty to me. I was turned on just by the sound of her voice.

"Hi," I said almost flirtatiously. "I just wanted to thank you for inviting me to the screening. I'm sorry that we passed on the soundtrack."

"I totally understand. No worries," she said. "I'm happy we got the opportunity to meet each other."

"Me, too. So, exactly what do you do?" I asked.

"I choose music for film," she said.

"What does that mean?"

"Well, I listen to tons of music and I try to set the scene in the film by playing songs against the picture until I find something that works," she said.

"That's a pretty cool job."

"Yeah. And when we have a soundtrack we contact record label execs like you to see if they're interested in releasing it."

"Cool. I don't know too much about the film side of the biz. But it sounds very interesting."

"Well, now that I think about it, I'm music supervising an independent film called *Far Harbor*. Keola Beamer does the score. He's a Hawaiian slack-key guitarist. It would actually be a perfect fit for Milan."

"Please send it over to me. Maybe we can do business together."

"It's so weird that you called me. I've been stressing for a week about finding a label to release the soundtrack, and then you called."

"Hmm. That is weird."

"I guess it's fate, huh?"

"When I get the package I'll call you back. Is that cool?"

I had no intention of listening to the soundtrack. I told her that I would listen to it because it gave me an excuse to call her again. I couldn't figure out why I was so interested in speaking with her. But there was something about her voice that made me feel safe, and all I could think about after that first telephone call was trying to find reasons to speak with her again and again and again.

Sadly, I couldn't do business with Lisa even if I wanted to. She may have thought that I was a big-time record exec, but I was far from it. My coke habit was hindering my ability to generate publicity for the record company's artist roster and soundtracks. I was supposed to be lining up interviews for Ryuichi Sakamoto, an avant-garde musician whose solo album, *Smoochy,* was being released by Milan in the spring of 1996. I had to get on the telephone and call music journalists at magazines like *Rolling Stone* and *Spin,* and music critics at papers like *The New York Times,* the *Boston Globe,* and the *Baltimore Chronicle,* send the writers advance copies of the albums, and try to get the albums reviewed in their publications. Another problem: I didn't know anyone who wrote for those publications. I had pretended that I did, telling my boss and everyone else I worked with that I had a Rolodex filled with A-list telephone numbers that I could use it to get journalists to write feature stories on the label and record reviews for the soundtracks.

I fell in love with Lisa on the telephone, without even remembering exactly what she looked like. She made it so easy. I spoke to her every day after our first conversation. The topics soon moved way beyond the soundtrack she was trying to hawk.

One night, I called Lisa from my office at 8:00 p.m. and spoke to her until nine the next morning. I cradled the phone on my shoulder and cut lines on my desk. Every couple of minutes I'd ask Lisa to hold on, and I'd snort some coke before jumping back into our conversation. The drug acted like a truth serum— sort of. I poured my heart out to Lisa over the telephone, but used the past tense when describing my drug addiction, my thievery, and the verbal and physical abuse I earned from my father by being incorrigible over the years. All of the other bad things I'd done that I could think of, I confessed to Lisa.

"I'm not like that anymore, though," I told her.

I thought that if Lisa could handle my dark side, if she didn't hang up the phone, then perhaps I could become the person I had just described to her. If that happened then maybe I'd have something to live for.

There was silence. I could hear Lisa breathe. I bit down on my hand. I was petrified, anticipating her reaction.

"I...I think I love you," Lisa said. I could tell she was a bit confused by her response, probably because she truly meant it and knew that in the real world it was quite unusual to fall in love with a person who you wouldn't be able to describe to a police sketch artist.

I loved her, too. I felt it in my gut, in my chest, in my hands. But I couldn't understand why she loved me.

"You may have done some bad things, but you have a good heart," she said.

We saw two different Jasons. Where she saw a kind person, I saw a bastard. Where she saw intellect I saw myself as uneducated. Innocent in her mind, deceptive in mine. So I cried silently. This all seemed like a fairy tale. This whirlwind romance seemed too perfect. But I so desperately wanted to live happily ever after.

"I need to see you."

I took a two-week vacation from work in March of 1996 and flew to Los Angeles to be with Lisa. I had an extra 400 CDs shipped to the record store the week before I left and used the two grand in cash to pay for the flight and the hotel. Lisa, still believing I was a big-time music exec, suggested I stay at the Peninsula Hotel in Beverly Hills. It was pretty pricey but, since I played the role of power broker, I agreed. I sold 200 more CDs and picked up another grand from the record store to cover the additional costs.

Lisa met me at the airport when I got to Los Angeles. She didn't look like the woman I had created in my mind, even though she told me a dozen times what she looked like. I realized, even in my mind's eye, I could be pretty shallow. I envisioned Lisa to be tall, blonde, big-breasted, with fuck-me pumps and garters. The real Lisa is five feet tall and looks like Shannen Doherty. Lisa is adorable and so tiny. I wanted to put her in my pocket. When Lisa spoke my heart beat faster. That voice! I was really in love with her. I mean really in love with her. I leaned down and gave her a kiss.

"I don't like what you're wearing," Lisa said, after she kissed me. "Can we please get you a new outfit?"

I wore Wrangler jeans, black motorcycle boots, a belt adorned with pieces of metal, a suede vest, and a white corduroy cowboy shirt.

"Why? What's wrong with this? I think I look cool," I said.

The first thing we did was go to Banana Republic where she picked out a new outfit for me.

Lisa and I spent the next two weeks mostly ordering room service at the Peninsula. She was my soul mate. I knew it the moment she called her grandmother to tell her about me. We were on our way to a restaurant. Lisa drove.

"Mama…"

She called her grandmother "Mama."

"Oh my God!" I said. "I call my grandmother 'Mama,' too! That's so weird!'"

I grabbed Lisa's right hand, forcing her to steer with her left, and held it tightly to my chest.

I thought that I was the only person in the world who used Mama and Papa instead of grandma and grandpa to identify my grandparents. I adored my Mama and Papa. They were Gods. They could do no wrong in my eyes. When I was younger I used to pray to God—literally—to keep Mama and Papa alive forever. Then I would stare at the palms of my hands for minutes and believe that my prayers would be answered.

Mama and Papa were born in Europe, and when the Nazis rose to power they were sent to a concentration camp in France along with my two uncles—Mama and Papa's sons—and escaped to the Dominican Republic in 1945, where Mama gave birth to my mother. Five years later, they moved to the United States, and in 1955 they settled in the Bronx. From what I know, most of my extended family on my mother's side was exterminated by the Nazis and most of my father's immediate family all died fairly young. So, aside from a few aunts and uncles that I barely saw, Mama and Papa were pretty much the only other relatives I had.

My family used to live around the corner from Mama and Papa in the Bronx, on Bogart Avenue, a street lined with massive tree trunks that had limbs that seemed to touch the heavens, and obscured the two-family brick dwellings that housed mostly other Jewish immigrants who also survived the Holocaust.

As far back as I can remember I spent every weekend at Mama and Papa's house. Had I been given a choice I never would have left.

It must have been a Friday or Saturday afternoon in 1970-something when my parents, my brother and sister got into my Mom's cherry red Cadillac convertible and left the suburbs, where we relocated a couple of years earlier, to visit Mama and Papa in the Bronx. At five or six years old I was already miserable with my home life. I couldn't wait to get to Mama and Papa's for my weekend getaway. Sitting in the backseat of my mother's car, I stared at my father's left arm resting on the headrest of my mother's seat. I was angry that he had joined us for the forty-minute ride.

When we arrived at Mama and Papa's I was the first one out of the car, climbing over my brother and sister, so I could race up the stairs and be the first one to greet them with a kiss. There were other grandkids on the block playing stickball and riding their bikes, but I never socialized with any of them. Spending every free moment with Mama and Papa was more important. Mama called me yingelah, and when they spoke to me it was mostly in Yiddish. They told me stories about the Holocaust, and how they survived the Nazi death camps. They taught me that life was about survival, particularly for a Jew. I'd like to think that their stories of endurance served me well.

Mama and Papa hugged my brother and sister and my parents and kissed all of them on both cheeks. When we walked inside the salty smell of homemade mushroom barley soup and potato knishes made my mouth water. Mama made her own iced tea, which was perfect because I liked it sweet and she wasn't afraid to add sugar. We sat at the kitchen table with Papa while Mama served all of us dinner and asked my mother how everything was in a tone that sounded worried.

"Fine, fine," my mother would say in Yiddish. "There's nothing to worry about. The house is good, the kids are good. We're fine."

When things were bad—real bad—we weren't allowed to tell Mama and Papa. My mother feared that bad news would cause Mama and Papa to have heart attacks and die. So even though I felt like shit, and was failing in school, and wanted to tell them that my father hit me whenever I got into trouble, I had to lie and pretend that my life was perfect.

My father rarely spoke to Mama and Papa. I think he sensed that they didn't like him very much because of his temper. They did, however, respect that he was a hard worker. Dad drove a cab in Manhattan. His cab was unlike any other. He displayed a strange and elaborate collection of tchotchkes on his dashboard that he bought from street vendors.

Dad was napping in the living room when Mom said I needed to ask him if I could spend the rest of the weekend at Mama and Papa's.

I hated asking my dad for anything. I feared that he would say no, and not getting what I wanted was something I was not equipped to deal with. Whenever I was forced to ask my dad for money, I acted like a little girl, tilting my head to one side, twirling my hair, and smiling.

"Daddy, daddy."

"Huh, huh, what is it? I'm sleeping."

"Mommy told me to ask you if I can stay here tonight and tomorrow."

"No. Not this week. No one can pick you up."

I wouldn't let up. I asked and asked, and came up with different ways I thought my dad would be able to swing by and pick me up even though it would have been a real inconvenience for him.

My whining annoyed the shit out of him. He slapped me across my face, and dragged me out to the front porch, shook me and slapped me again. I peed my pants. Having witnessed this, Mama and Papa's neighbors grabbed their grandkids by the wrist and dragged them inside. I don't remember seeing Papa grab my father's arm, but I do recall seeing my father punch Papa in the jaw, knocking him out. My mother scooped me up and put me in the backseat of her car and went back into Mama and Papa's to grab my sister, who was just a baby. My father didn't set foot in Mama and Papa's house again for five years.

Lisa and I talked about spending the rest of our lives together. We spent the next three months traveling between New York and Los Angeles to be with each other. But I lived a double life and was still selling CDs and delivering cash to Lenny every month and snorting tiny mountains of cocaine at night, alone, in my studio apartment. I didn't have any furniture. I didn't even own a lamp. I slept on an inflatable mattress that was half dead. About this time, I started to experience cocaine-induced delusions in the form of giant rats that caused me to strip off my clothes and burn the flesh on my legs with cigarette butts. Even though Lisa swore to me over and over that she loved me unconditionally, I couldn't bring myself to admit to her that I continued to snort coke, and there was no way in hell that I was going to tell her that I was stealing CDs from Milan to pay a couple of goombahs. The more our love grew, the more ashamed I was at what I had become.

I was in Los Angeles, spending the weekend at Lisa's parents' house, that Friday morning in May 1996 when I got the call from Milan's CEO telling me I was fired.

"You screwed up everything on the Ryuichi Sakamoto album," the CEO told me. "You lied. You didn't service the album to journalists. John called to follow up. No one got it. I am so disappointed in you."

"I'm sorry. Please don't fire me. I'm so sorry," I said, sobbing, over the telephone in Lisa's bedroom. "You're like family to me. Don't fire me."

"I'm sorry, Jason."

Pathetic. I'm not sure if I was crying because I was genuinely upset about losing my job, or whether I started having regrets about sabotaging my career, or if I was consumed with guilt, or if I was just relieved that it was all over. Fuck it. This was a sign, I thought. I could move to California and start over. Get another label job. Clean slate. Move away from the drugs. Move away from my fucked-up family. Lisa doesn't do drugs. She doesn't even drink alcohol. Being with her will keep me clean and sober.

"I'm so sorry for you," Lisa said, having overheard my conversation with the CEO. I didn't tell Lisa the truth. I told her I was fired from Milan because Ryuichi Sakamoto's manager didn't like me, that I was unable to get Sakamoto into *Rolling Stone*, and that his manager threatened to bring the record to another label unless Milan got rid of me. I totally played the victim and she bought it.

"I wanna go to the beach," I told Lisa. "Do you mind? Can we go there?"

"Good idea."

Lisa let me drive her car. I didn't have a driver's license. It was suspended in 1989. She didn't know that.

Our fingers were intertwined as we walked barefoot on the sand at the beach in Santa Monica. I walked into the Pacific Ocean for the first time. I submerged myself in the water. It was salty and warm. I turned around and saw the Santa Monica Mountains in the distance. There were palm trees everywhere. I loved palm trees. They made me feel reborn, like I didn't have to think about my past or my fucked-up life back in New York. It made everything seem so far away. I realized there was no other place in the world I wanted to be. Spontaneously, I asked Lisa if she would marry me.

"Yes!" she said without even thinking. Years later, when I asked her why she said yes, she told me, "It just felt right."

I went back to my apartment in New York and put all of my belongings into two garbage bags. I told my landlord I was moving to California to get married and said she could keep my security deposit to cover the rent for June. I withdrew all my money from the bank, 2,200.84 dollars. I called the CEO at Milan and asked him if I could stop by to clean out my desk.

"Yes. I think it's important we move on," he said.

Everyone at Milan was genuinely happy to see me. I told them I was going to move to California at the end of June to get married.

"We'll miss you," John said.

I left Milan's offices and took a subway back to my apartment. I called my parents.

"I got big news," I said to my mother. "I'm coming home."

"Oy yoy yoy. What is it? Are you hurt? Is everything okay?"

"Yes. Everything is fine."

"You almost gave me a heart attack. Wh…wh…what is it? What do you need to tell me? Are you sure everything is okay? You didn't break any bones?"

"I'll tell you when I get home. I'm fine."

I planned on leaving New York City forever in three weeks, at the end of June 1996. I avoided contact with Maury and Lenny and Bruno and everyone else at the Pit Stop. I was going to hide out in my parents' house in upstate New York until I left for California. I remembered, however, that I gave Lenny my passport—which listed my parents' address—when he told me nearly a year ago that I had to sell CDs for him. I started to fear that Lenny was going to send a bunch of mugs to kill me.

I call my sister, Michelle, and asked her to do me a favor and call Maury at the Pit Stop.

"Why can't you call?" she asked.

"I don't want him to know where I am."

"Why not?"

"Because. That's why. Can you do it?"

"What am I supposed to say?"

"Tell him that I'm in a mental hospital for trying to commit suicide."

"What! What the fuck are you talking about? Why should I say that?"

"Just do it. Please?"

Michelle, God love her, said she'd make the call for twenty bucks, no questions asked. I gave her the number to the bar.

"Call me after you call him."

Michelle called me back five minutes later.

"What'd he say?" I asked her.

"He said he loves you, that everyone there loves you, but you owe someone a lot of money and there's nothing he can do."

"That's it?"

"Uh-huh. Who do you owe money to?"

"No one. I don't know what he's talking about."

That night I told my family I was moving to California to marry Lisa. They had met her once at a dinner in Manhattan, when Lisa came to New York to visit me.

"Great. Mazel Tov," my father said, dryly. "You get her a ring?"

"No."

"No? You gotta give her a ring."

"She doesn't want one."

It was true. Lisa told me her grandmother, who passed away years earlier, gave her a ring surrounded with diamonds that she could use as an engagement ring when someone proposed to her. *That's cool*, I thought, 'cause I didn't have money for a ring.

"How do you ask someone to marry you without giving them a ring?" my father asked, clearly annoyed by my lack of etiquette.

"Well, I did and she said yes."

"It's not right," my father said as he got up from the kitchen table and walked into his bedroom to take a nap.

My mother became emotional—not about my engagement, but that I was going to move to California.

"You're gonna leave me?" she asked.

"No. I'm leaving New York," I said, somewhat sarcastically.

"You don't think you'll change your mind and stay here?"

"No way."

"So you are leaving me." My mother started to cry and the thick, black mascara and eyeliner encrusted on her eyelashes melted all over her face. She too got up and went to her bedroom. This is exactly the reason I wanted to get out of New York. I hated my family. They drove me nuts with their drama.

Three days before I was supposed to split for Los Angeles, I got a call from a woman named Jennifer who I worked with at Milan. She was lanky and had a long face like a horse. I'd known her for about five years and had gotten her a job at Milan after she was laid off from another label. We worked together doing publicity and promotion for Milan, but Jennifer actually did real work while I slacked off and embezzled from the label.

"Hey, Jason," Jennifer said.

"Hey, what's up?"

"When are you leaving?"

"Saturday."

"Listen, a bunch of us are down here at Sticky Mike's Frog Bar on 8th Avenue and we wanna get you fucked up before you leave. Can you meet us?"

"Yeah. Definitely. I'll be down there in a couple of hours."

"Cool. We'll be in the back."

"Okay. See ya later."

Perfect. I wanted to score some coke in the city for the last time anyway. I got a friend of mine to give me a ride for fifteen dollars. He dropped me off on 41st and 8th. I was going to take the subway to a different bar, on 14th and 6th, to buy coke and then meet the gang at Sticky Mike's. For some reason or another, I decided to go to Sticky Mike's first.

It was packed. The music was excruciatingly loud. I fought my way to the back of the bar. I looked around. No sign of Jennifer. I turned around and leaned up on the tips of my toes to see if she was sitting at a table at the front of the bar. I didn't see her. I turned around again and surveyed the back of the bar one more time. I felt a tap on my shoulder. I spun around.

"NYPD Detective," said the Latino man in the suit, shoving his badge up against my nose, "put your hands behind your back and don't try to run."

Another detective came up behind me, grabbed my arms, and held my wrists together. I felt the cold steel of handcuffs being slapped on my wrists. Click-click-click-click. The feeling and sound were familiar. I'd been in and out of trouble since I was five years old. That's when my parents first busted me for stealing my friend's Matchbox cars. I quickly graduated to digging through my mother's friends' purses and stealing cash out of their wallets. When I was in my teens, I stole my mother's jewelry and hocked it. In high school, I broke into other students' lockers and stole all sorts of shit. As I got older, I became more daring and started pulling off credit card scams and other petty crimes and got caught a bunch of times. I wish I could come up with a good reason for the stealing, like I had a family to feed or something, but to tell you the truth I did it because I knew I would get away with it. I got off on probation, and the arrests were eventually expunged from my record. But I knew this was a serious one.

I took the perp walk through the bar. The detectives were on both sides of me, holding on to my biceps. All I could think of at that moment was thank God I didn't go to the other bar first and buy coke. I would've really been fucked if those Five-O's found drugs on me. My heart was beating like a Neal Peart drum solo. Everything around me happened in slow motion. By the time the detectives shoved me into the backseat of their unmarked cruiser that was parked across the street from the bar I felt like I had been walking for miles. Then it hit me. Jennifer. That fucking bitch. She set me up. The detective read me my Miranda rights.

"You understand these rights?" he asked.

"Mmm-hmm," I said.

When I got to the police station the Latino detective brought me into his office and searched me.

"You don't have any sharp objects in your pockets I'm gonna cut myself with, do ya?" the detective asked.

"No. Just a money clip. And about 200 dollars."

Lisa had bought a money clip for me from Tiffany's when I was out in L.A. because I carried around wads of cash.

The detective laid out the charge against me: grand theft larceny. I'd been charged with stealing 900 CDs from Milan.

He said they'd been investigating me for six months and had a videotape of me from the security camera, dragging a suitcase out of the building in the wee hours of the morning one Thursday night in July 1995. He said they could prove the suitcase contained the CDs Milan reported stolen the next day.

"We got the CDs from the record stores you sold 'em at," the detective said.

"Oh yeah?" I said. I don't know how they came up with 900 CDs. I only sold 450 that day. John, my ex-coworker, must have given the cops the wrong amount.

"We also got a guy you sold 'em to," the detective said, "He says he could identify you."

Much to my surprise, the detectives didn't mention anything about my bigger scam: the thousands of CDs I had shipped directly to another record store on Bleecker Street for nearly a year. That accusation would come much later, when the Manhattan District Attorney would tell my defense lawyer that he was prepared to amend the charges against me, alleging I stole 20,000 or so CDs from Milan over the past two and one-half years, defrauding the company out of half a million dollars. Damn. Could I have stolen that much swag? If I did, I had nothing to show for it except for the tender lining on the inside of my nose. Nobody ever mentioned Lenny or Bruno. I certainly didn't utter a word about my association with them. In fact, I never heard from or saw either of them again after I got arrested.

The black detective said nothing. The Latino detective did all of the talking. If I knew then what I know now about cops and the tactics they use to get suspects to confess, I would have kept my mouth shut. How was I supposed to know that the first time in my life I decided to come clean and tell the truth it would backfire? I told the Latino detective that I was supposed to move to Los Angeles in two days to get married.

"Admit that you stole the CDs and then you can leave," the detective said. "You can write an apology note to your ex-boss saying you're sorry for what you did, promise to pay him back and that you'll never do it again. It's your choice."

I wish I had (a) asked for a lawyer and (b) known that the Latino detective was coercing me into a confession and making empty promises, which, in the eyes of the law, is perfectly legal. (I would, however, use those same manipulative law enforcement tactics years later in order to extract info out of my sources and land some of the biggest newspaper scoops of 2000 and 2001.) All I could think about when the detective was laying it out for me was Lisa and how badly I wanted to be with her. I believed if I copped to my crime—not all of it, but just the night in question—I'd walk out of the police station that night a free man.

"Okay. I did it," I said, "I stole the CDs. It was me."

The Latino detective looked at his black partner and smirked, a facial expression I remember vividly, though it would take years for me to realize what it meant. They got me.

"I'll be right back," the Latino detective said. "In the meantime, here's a pad and a pen. Write down exactly what you did, when you did it, and how you did it. Then sign and date it."

I confessed. I wrote down that I stole the 900 CDs from Milan that night even though it was only 450. *Soon I'll be with Lisa*, I thought. As I summarized my crime, I actually felt a sense of honor about taking responsibility for my actions. *Redemption is good*, I thought. But I would soon regret it.

The detective came back into the office about ten minutes later. He had some papers for me to sign.

"I just need you to sign this," he said. "It says that your admission was not forced by me and you did it voluntarily."

"Okay. Where do I sign?" I asked.

"Here, and here."

I signed the paperwork and stood up.

"Can I leave now?"

"Not quite," the detective said. "You mind sitting in a lineup?"

"What for?" I asked, naively.

"We got the guy from the record store here," the detective said. "He says he could pick you out. It's just a formality. You already confessed."

I wondered which guy was going to rat on me. There were so many stores in Manhattan I sold CDs to. I'm sure the cops threatened to file criminal charges against the storeowner for buying the CDs from me unless he cooperated with their investigation of me.

"Fine. I'll do the lineup," I said.

The detective put me in a small room. I sat on a chair facing a one-way mirror. It wasn't the type of lineup you see in the movies, where suspects stand against a cement wall with a banner behind their backs that says how tall they are. This was just a plain white room. Four men, who I assume were supposed to have similar features to mine, came into the room and sat on the chairs next to me. They must have been cops. We sat there and stared at the one-way mirror. About thirty seconds later the detective came in and told the other guys to leave.

"Our guy picked you," he said, proudly.

He put me in a holding cell. I had no idea what was going on.

Two hours later, the Latino detective let me out of the cell. His black partner slapped the cuffs on me again and both of them escorted me to their unmarked cruiser.

85

"Where are we going?" I asked.

"We gotta take you downtown," the black detective told me, "to central booking."

"Why?"

"'Cause we're charging you."

"Whadda ya mean? I thought you said I could go?"

"Nope. You gotta be arraigned first."

"But I'm supposed to go to California on Saturday. I'm gonna get married."

"I don't think you're gonna make it. You'll probably be in jail for a few days before the arraignment."

"Jail? Oh please don't take me to jail. Please, please, please, please. No jail."

I was petrified of going to jail, fearing that a skinny, long-haired white guy like me would become some big black guy's bitch. I had no idea what to expect. I was scared shitless.

"Gotta do it," the detective said. "You'll be fine. Just stay close to the guards."

"What kind of people are gonna be there?"

"Rapists, murderers, bangers," the detective said, "all types of lowlifes."

The black detective was having fun scaring the fucking bejesus out of me.

We stopped off at a deli before they dropped me off at Central Booking. The black detective said he'd buy me a pack of cigarettes and a chocolate bar. He reached into my pants pocket and took a five dollar bill.

I got dropped off at a place called The Tombs. Everyone who's arrested in Manhattan goes there before they see the judge. This was no friendly doctor's waiting room. The Tombs is the largest prisoner receiving area in the country. It was built in

1835 on swampy land that used to be a lake called The Collect. It got its creepy name when the architect, after returning to New York from a trip to Egypt, modeled the jail after a mausoleum he saw there.

The guard who admitted me took my cash and money clip, but said I could keep my chocolate bar. The black detective unlocked the handcuffs. I massaged my wrists. The Latino detective gave me a salute, not out of respect, more like he was saying, "Ha, ha, loser," and then both detectives left.

I asked the prison guard if I could make my one phone call.

"Take a number," he said, "you got 500 people in front of you."

He put me in a holding cell that gave new meaning to the phrase "sardines in a can." I stood, like a soldier, with my arms to my side and my feet together next to a hundred other inmates because the cell was so small. They packed us in so tightly that there was no room to get comfortable. I thought about being a wise ass and saying something to the guard, thinking that maybe my humor would go over well with the other prisoners and keep me safe from the possibility of being roughed up. But I kept my mouth shut.

None of the other inmates taunted me. I gave one my chocolate bar because he was going through major heroin withdrawals, shaking like a leaf on a tree, begging the prison guard for something sweet to eat. It took four days before I finally got my phone call. I suppose most people would have used their only phone call to contact someone who can get them sprung from jail, but I used mine to call Lisa in California.

I was going to say goodbye. Lisa barely knew me. Already I was in jail. I dialed her number.

"Lisa?" I said, my voice quivering.

"Jason! Oh my God! Are you okay?"

"I'm sorry, Lisa," I said, "I'm sorry."

"Jason, I know everything that's going on," she said, "My dad is trying to get you an attorney. We're gonna get you out of jail."

"You still wanna be with me?" I asked in my little kid voice. "Of course I do," she said. "I love you."

The guard took the phone out of my hand and hung it up.

I couldn't believe Lisa still loved me. There was no way in hell my father would support my sister if she told him her boyfriend of three months was in jail. In fact, I don't think there are many fathers or mothers on the face of the planet who would stand by their child's boyfriend who was locked up like I was after they've been dating for such a short time. I don't think there are many girlfriends in this world that would do that, either.

I was assigned a public defender. He asked me a bunch of questions about my crime and gave me a cigarette.

We appeared before the judge together. I think it was about 5:30 a.m. "How do you plead to these charges, Mr. Leopold?" the judge asked. "Not guilty, your honor," I said.

The judge set bail at five thousand dollars; the district attorney had told him I was a flight risk because of my "connections" in California. I leaned over to my public defender and whispered in his ear, "I don't have any money. Tell the judge that I work in the music business. I have connections to California as well as many other states."

The public defender relayed the information to the judge and tossed in a lie I told him about graduating from NYU. The judge thought about it for a minute.

"Okay," the judge said, "I'll release you, but you are not permitted to travel out of the state."

"Thank you, your honor," I said.

I ran out of the courtroom. I didn't even say goodbye to my public defender. When I got outside I got down on my knees and kissed the filthy fucking New York City sidewalk. I took the bus home to my parents' house and told them that I was set up, wrongfully accused of robbing my company.

"Oh," I said. "I'm moving to California tonight. Can you drive me to the airport?"

I defied the judge's order. I had no intention of sticking around in New York. I needed Lisa.

My parents were in a state of shock. They never had a chance to absorb what happened because I had packed everything I owned into a duffle bag and was ready to go. Soon I was on a plane headed for California. Lisa met me at the airport.

"Lisa," I said, "I can't believe you still want to be with me. I don't understand why."

"I just love you," she said. "I can't explain it."

Lisa was still living at home, and the next morning I had to face her parents. I was dreading it. Who wouldn't? But Lisa said it was important to her.

"We don't keep any secrets in our family," she said.

I walked to the backyard and Lisa's mother, Terry, and father, Phil, were lounging by the pool. I gave her mother a kiss on the cheek and shook Phil's hand. Then I took a seat next to them. I was nervous. I started to bite my nails.

Terry said she wanted Lisa and me to take our relationship really slow. She was worried about what Lisa was about to get herself into. I could see the worry on her face. Phil asked me about my life. He wanted to know everything about me. I gave him the same cock-and-bull story I gave Lisa, and my parents. I was the victim. I'm Job. Bad things happen to me. I'd been set up. In fact, I lied so convincingly that I believed my own bullshit. They seemed to feel sorry for me and genuinely wanted to help me, something I wasn't used to. It was six years later when I finally took responsibility and looked them in the eyes and came clean. They said matter-of-factly, "Oh, we knew."

Lisa and I moved into an apartment about two weeks later, and except for a few episodes, I stopped drinking and using. I had to fly back and forth to New York to deal with the case. Like an idiot, I thought I could still work in the music industry. I didn't think anyone in California would know about the shit that happened in New York with Milan. I set up a half-dozen interviews at some record labels. The first words out of everyone's mouth were, "So I hear you got arrested for stealing CDs from Milan and selling them."

I was blacklisted. No one would hire me. The news about my arrest was all over the industry.

I needed money to help pay the rent, so I took a job in a bookstore for five bucks an hour. I fucking hated it. Retail sucks. The last retail job I worked was at Tower Records in Manhattan, where I was fired for beating up a customer. The customer was actually my ex-girlfriend's new boyfriend, who came into the store to taunt me. I lost it. I hopped over the counter and grabbed him and just started whaling on him. Next day I got a call from the store manager.

"Jason, we can't have our employees beating up our customers," he said. "I'm gonna have to let you go."

Then I pursued my fallback career, journalism. I had some decent clips from the *Reporter Dispatch*, my first writing job, at a daily paper in White Plains. They were a couple of years old. I didn't have any fresh ones. I typed up a resume, omitting Milan and replaced it with the name of my brother's home improvement company. I called every newspaper listed in the yellow pages. I asked to speak with the managing editors. I scored an interview at the *Whittier Daily News*. They were looking for a cops and courts reporter. I had a lot of experience with that.

The managing editor of the paper's parent company also interviewed me.

"You know why your name sounds familiar to me?" he asked.

"Uh-uh. Why?"

"Because you called every person at this paper looking for a job," he said. "You're pretty aggressive, huh?"

"Yeah," I said. "Sorry about that."

"Sorry?" he said. "What are you talking about? We need an aggressive reporter for the cop beat. Trust me. You'll go far in this business if you're aggressive."

I got hired at the *Whittier Daily News* in February of 1997, seven months after I moved to Los Angeles. I never went back to the bookstore. I never quit and I never even bothered to pick up my last check.

I got a notice from the DA in New York. He sent it to my parents' house and they forwarded it to me in Los Angeles. They were amending the charges against me. They were going to prove that I had stolen more than 20,000 CDS. If I decided to fight the charges and was found guilty, my lawyer said I could be sent to prison for fifteen years. I imagined getting repeatedly raped. There's no way I could do fifteen years.

"Jason, the DA's offering us a deal," said my criminal attorney. "They won't make you do any time, but you gotta plead guilty to a Class E felony of grand theft and pay some restitution. You'll also be on probation for five years and you'll have to report to a probation officer."

"What about the felony?" I asked. "Does that mean I can't vote?"

"Yeah," said the attorney. "And you can't get Social Security. But it's a Class E. It's no big deal. Don't you want to get on with your life? Get married to Lisa?"

I discussed the options with Lisa and her parents. We all thought that this was a sweet deal and that it would give me the closure I needed to move on with my life. Two months after I accepted the plea bargain, Lisa and I got married.

Six months later, I started drinking again. Then I started to crave cocaine.

FIVE

I WAS TOO MENTALLY UNSTABLE to work at the regional newswire City News. I know that now. I should have been in counseling, dealing with the impact of my felony on my marriage and the flashbacks that kept coming back to haunt me. Instead, I lived a double life. I spent the six months I worked at City News drowning myself in alcohol and cocaine. Nobody had a clue. Not my wife, my friends, or my editors.

City News Service is a regional news wire that covers Southern California. It has reporters staffed in bureaus at courthouses and police stations and City Hall, like a miniature Associated Press. Most of its subscribers were other media outlets, including AP, *Los Angeles Times*, *Hollywood Reporter*, and *Variety*, who all looked upon City News as a tip service. When a reporter for City News filed a breaking news story, a reporter at a television station or a paper would make a few additional calls and incorporate the City News report as if it were their own—but City News had a reputation for getting facts wrong. Many reporters who worked for City News were fresh out of college, and they were often forced to sacrifice accuracy for speed. That's why newspapers or television stations in Los Angeles or San Diego would not reprint a City News story.

Still, City News was a breeding ground for some of Los Angeles' most respected journalists. Bill Boyarsky, the former city editor and columnist at the *Times*, started there. City News had a reputation for long hours and low pay. Sometimes you'd find yourself writing six stories a day and rewriting a story a dozen times as it developed. You couldn't buy that experience in school.

I worked in an old pressroom on the second floor of the downtown Los Angeles civil courthouse building. It looked like a museum. Vintage Royal typewriters were stacked in a corner covered with cobwebs; yellowed newspapers from the 1940s and 1950s were plastered on the walls. In a rear corner stood a dusty bar that hadn't been stocked in ages. And in the middle of the room was a threadbare couch that shed fibers like a balding man. It all looked like a private investigator's office from a 1950s pulp serial. It also resembled the *Mary Tyler Moore Show* newsroom—thin wood paneling and fiberglass door windows with peeling decals identifying the news organization. The door nearest me said C ty News S rvic.

I shared the pressroom with some hack from *Entertainment Tonight*, a young female reporter from a legal newspaper, the *Daily Journal*, and a guy who made a living searching courthouse files for newsy lawsuits, which he then copied and sold to out-of-state attorneys. My City News Service editors, Lori and Pat, worked out of a high-rise office building ten miles away in Century City; thankfully, my only communication with them was over the telephone. Lori and Pat personified the stereotypical rude, obnoxious, cranky, and egotistical editors. They would sometimes call me after I finished a story to insult me with questions just to prove a point.

"So I understand you found a new spelling for 'plaintiff,'" said Pat in a twangy Midwestern accent, without wasting time with a greeting. He always spoke over a speakerphone, and I'd get to hear his insults while he clacked at his keyboard editing my stories.

"Does this new spelling of 'plaintiff' appear in the Oxford Dictionary?"

"So I spelled it wrong?"

"I'm not saying it's wrong. If 'plaintiff' is now spelled with one F then I want to make sure you send me a memo on it."

I took everything Pat said personally. My emotions had been rubbed raw from the felony conviction I received a few months earlier. There was a war going on inside my head, and at that point I blamed my mother and father for all of it.

There are times I'm sure I deserved physical discipline from my father. I provoked him, and the only way he knew how to administer punishment was with his fists. He wasn't one of those parents who came home from work, hit the bottle, and beat his kids. To get whacked, you had to give him a reason.

◇

ONE PARTICULAR MEMORY HAUNTED me for years.

When I got a driver's license, my father bought me a new car, a Ford Tempo sport edition. It was sky blue, with aluminum alloy wheels and a four-cylinder, five-speed engine. Though my dad claims he bought me the car, somehow I wound up doling out the monthly payments, which I earned from pumping gas part-time.

The restrictions my father put on the car were many. I wasn't allowed to drive the car to school because my father feared vandalism. I wasn't allowed to carry passengers in the car; my dad said that insurance wouldn't cover them. I was only allowed to drive the car on weekends—not for pleasure, but to get to work, just a mile and a half away from our house.

But the temptation to explore my small town and impress chicks with my new set of wheels was too great to resist.

Two feet of snow covered the ground the morning I decided to take my car out for a joy ride. The bitter cold air turned roads into a sheet of ice and it was too dangerous for the school buses to make the rounds. School was cancelled. I owned the day. My father left for work at 7:00 a.m. and wouldn't return for thirteen hours, giving me plenty of time to pick up my friends and drive to the Nanuet Mall to impress the ladies. A couple hours after my father and mother left for work I phoned a half-dozen of my friends.

"You wanna like go to the mall and pick up some chicks?"

"Umm, I don't like wanna stand outside at the bus stop. It's too cold."

"Let's drive there. I'm going to take my car."

Five of my friends squeezed into the backseat of the Tempo. Ron sat in the front.

"Jace, check it out dude. Wanna smoke a bowl?" My friend Scott took out a baggie half-filled with weed. He had a glass pipe neatly decorated with blotches of three different colors and stuffed a wad of grass into the bowl and handed it to me. I held it to my lips with my right hand while another friend flicked the lighter to burn the weed. I held the smoke in my lungs as long as I could. Smoke danced around and lingered inside of the car.

"Dude. I am lit," I said. "Let's stop at White Castle."

The snow continued to fall from the sky in what seemed like slow motion. I performed a few tricks with the car on the powder—mostly fishtails and donuts—in the parking lot of

Nanuet Mall. We spent three hours at the mall playing video games and left without meeting any chicks. I dropped my friends off and parked the Tempo exactly where it was left before I backed it out of my driveway that morning. I went inside and took a nap. About four hours later my father woke me up, shouting from the house's entryway: "Jason! Jason! Get down here. NOW."

"Ahh shit," I said to myself, as I walked over to the staircase.

"Did you take the car out?" he asked.

"No."

"No?" He asked, making sure that was my final answer.

"Nope," I said.

"Do you think I'm some kind of idiot? There's snow packed inside the wheel well of the car. That means it was driven. On top of that, the tire tracks on the driveway match the tires on your car. I'm gonna knock your teeth in, you son of a bitch."

My father starts after me. I race down the stairs as he runs up the other set of stairs and grabs a shoe and throws it. I beg him to stop. "Leave me alone. I didn't do anything." He starts laughing in a sinister, *I'm going to get you* sort of way. Now I run to the screen door to escape, but it's locked. Anticipating my escape, Dad must have locked it when he first came in.

My hands start shaking as I feel for the button to unlock the screen door. Suddenly I find it, and WHAM! My head is slammed into the doorjamb. Father grabs a fistful of hair, pulls my head up, and slams it into the wall. Then he grabs my ear, dragging me outdoors. I fall onto the snow, but he still has a strong grip and I stumble to get on my feet.

"You still gonna lie to me about the car? Huh?" my father says, tormenting the defeated. I break free from his grip and run up the driveway.

"You fucking bastard. I'm gonna call the police. Fuck you!" I say. My father starts to run after me but I'm too fast for him outdoors. I don't have shoes on. My socks are packed with snow. My feet go numb. Still, I run. I touch my head. Something huge and smooth comes out of the side of my forehead. When I press my finger on it I get a brain freeze, the same kind you get if you drink a Slurpee too quickly.

I don't know why I have these horrible flashbacks, but they happen so frequently that I contemplate suicide. I can't deal with the pain from having to relive it all again. I decide I have no choice but to stop speaking to my parents.

"Jaaaayyyson? It's me. Why haven't you called," my mother asked me in her whiny voice.

"Um, I dunno. I've been busy."

"You're so busy that you can't find a few minutes to call and see how we are? You know how much that hurts me?"

"You wanna know why I haven't called?" I said. "Because every time I speak to you or Dad I get these flashbacks of when Dad hit me."

"What? What are you talking about? What hitting?" she said, playing dumb.

"You know. When I was little and when I was in high school," I said.

"Jason, that was so long ago. Don't you think it's time to move on?"

"I don't think I can talk to you or Dad anymore."

I wanted my mother to apologize for letting the abuse happen. I wanted her to fight for me. But she was cold and hung up, and I held the receiver until I heard a dial tone.

I also hoped my dad would call and say something like, "Jason, mom said you don't want to talk to me anymore. What's going on? Let's try and work this out."

I checked my machine obsessively for that message for two years, but it never came.

◇

I SPENT ALL OF the money I earned at City News on liquor and drugs. I explained these purchases to Lisa as money spent on car repairs and student loan payments. At night, I would tell Lisa I was working late at the office, and instead go to a heavy metal restaurant-bar on Sunset Boulevard to buy coke from the bartender and pay 150 dollars to rent the VIP room upstairs. I would snort lines off the table with complete strangers. The coke and alcohol made me forget about my felony, my parents, even Lisa. I didn't care about anything but getting high and making sure that I went to work so I would have money to buy more coke.

I wish I had had the capacity to tell my wife that I was fucked up, that I still felt an incredible amount of pain despite the fact that our starting a new life in Los Angeles was supposed to take all of that away.

When the psychotic attacks started I concocted a story so Lisa wouldn't become suspicious and figure out I was doing blow. But she knew something was up.

"Lisa! Lisa! Wake up."

"What! What is it?"

"Did you feel that?"

"Feel what?"

"Under the covers. I just felt something crawling on my leg. I think it's a rat."

Lisa jumped out of bed. She was also terrified of rats. My fear was so convincing. She lifted the blanket off the bed. Nothing.

"There's nothing there, Jason."

"I just felt something. Check again."

"See," she said, gliding her hand across the sheets. "There's nothing there. You're having a panic attack."

Lisa believed that the felony conviction and the fact that I cut off all contact with my parents played a pivotal role in my psychotic episodes. But as my coke addiction and my subsequent fear of the invisible rats became worse she started to sleep on the couch. One night, while she was sound asleep, I snorted a fat line of coke in the bathroom. About ten minutes later I ran down the stairs, drool coming out of my mouth and tried to wake her up.

"Lisa! Wake up! Rats! On me!"

The coke impaired my speech. I sounded like a stroke victim.

"Get away from me! I have to go to work tomorrow. Get away! I can't deal with this. Let me sleep!"

I was so paranoid, I could not snap out of it. I went into the kitchen, grabbed a steak knife from the drawer and started to slice open my arm, hoping it would shock me into reality. It didn't do a damn thing. Despite the fact that I was driving my wife further and further away from me, I could not stop snorting coke. I'd have the same psychotic episode every night for close to a year, and then attempt to wake Lisa up from a dead sleep. I was killing her. I was killing myself. There will never be enough apologies or flowers or diamonds in my life to express how truly sad and sorry I am for what I did to Lisa emotionally during that dark, dark year.

Nobody at work seemed to notice anything unusual about my behavior when I was high. I was amped up and speedy most of the day, but everyone thought that was from the four shots of espresso I drank every morning. The coke actually made me work harder during the day. I broke the news that Garry

Shandling had sued his former manager, Bernie Brillstein, for a hundred million dollars while I was flying on coke.

On a daily basis, I would thumb through hundreds of civil suits at the courthouse looking for anything newsworthy. I found a lawsuit a woman filed against a funeral home, claiming an embalmer butchered her dead daughter's hair, forcing the mother to put a wig on the corpse. I wrote the story up and got an e-mail from Pat that said, "Good digging. Great story."

During my lunch break, I would sit in the bathroom stall of the courthouse cutting lines of coke on the toilet seat. I kept a damp handkerchief in my back pocket and wiped my nose when the coke would start to crust around my nostrils. I wiped my nose so much that the skin around my nostrils started to chafe and peel.

Then Hunter Tylo, a stunning brunette who was a regular on the soap opera *The Bold and the Beautiful*, sued Aaron Spelling, the multimillionaire producer of *Beverly Hills, 90210*, for kicking her off of *Melrose Place* because she got pregnant. That trial cost me my job.

Activist attorney Gloria Allred supported Tylo's contention of wrongful termination and Spelling's attorneys argued that Tylo signed a contract that gave Spelling the power to fire her if there was any material change in her appearance. Pregnancy, Spelling's attorney's argued, fell into that category.

Covering the trial was easy. I started each day snorting caterpillar-sized lines in the bathroom stall inside the court pressroom. That kept me going until noon, when court broke for lunch and I would return to the stall to feed my coke addiction and follow that up with shots of whisky. I sprayed Calvin Klein cologne all over my body and swallowed large quantities of Listerine so no one could smell the bourbon. But it wasn't my drug and alcohol use that got me fired from City News.

On December 22, 1997, the jury ruled in favor of Tylo, awarding her the five million dollars. Curious what the pundits would say about the month-long trial, I stood next to the television cameras and listened to interviews. Stan Goldman, a legal analyst for Fox News during the O.J. Simpson trial, often appeared at celebrity trials to give his point of view on the proceedings. I approached him after he wrapped up an interview he gave to his own network.

"Mr. Goldman, hi, I'm Jason Leopold, a reporter for City News Service. What's your opinion on why Spelling's attorneys lost this case?"

Goldman gave me a perfect quote stating that Spelling's camp made a tactical mistake early on. I closed my story with Goldman's quote, knowing that it would infuriate Spelling's attorneys if they ever read it. After the story was posted, I went into the bathroom and snorted another couple of lines. Then I went to the bar to party.

The paper I briefly worked at before City News, the *Whittier Daily News*, picked up my story on the Tylo verdict and also ran the story in two of their other papers, the *Pasadena Star-News* and the *San Gabriel Valley Tribune*, the following morning. Two weeks after the story ran, Pat got a letter from Spelling's attorney, who just happened to live in Pasadena and read my story in the *Star-News*. He threatened to sue City News for defamation and libel. He said Goldman's quote "mischaracterized his trial experience."

Pat called me the day he got the letter.

"You fucked up, Leopold," Pat said. "Spelling's attorney is demanding we retract the quote about him in the Tylo story and he wants an apology to run on the wire."

"Pat, how did I fuck up? You edited my story. You didn't say anything about the quote then."

"Leopold, I edit fifty stories a day. I don't remember that quote," he said. "You should have stuck to what was said inside the courtroom."

"I don't see what the big deal is. It's not like I was editorializing. Goldman's the one who said it. He's the legal expert. He gave me his opinion"

"Well, it is a big deal. These guys have lots of money and they can afford to sue us. We're not a big operation like the *Los Angeles Times* where we can afford an expensive trial."

"Are you saying that you're going to run a correction? I didn't do anything wrong."

"This can hurt City News' credibility and we can't afford that. Send me your notes and the quotes you copied down from Goldman. We're going to see what our lawyers think."

I faxed copies of my notes to Pat and went into the bathroom to snort a few lines. My coke habit was getting worse. I was spending more time in the bathroom than at my desk. I started neglecting my work and sneaking out of the office earlier to go to the bar.

Pat called me a week later said that City News would run a correction across the wire. He said he spoke to the managing editor in charge of the *Whittier Daily News*, the *Pasadena Star-News*, and the *San Gabriel Valley Tribune*, and those papers would also print the correction.

"I can't believe you're caving in," I told Pat.

"Jason, I don't think you understand what libel is. I want you to come up to the Century City office after work today so we can talk," he said.

I knew that Pat was going to fire me. I had a gut feeling. But I thought that news organizations backed up their reporters and put up a fight when they were threatened with lawsuits. Before I left to meet Pat, the correction came over the wire.

Jason Leopold

Advisory, Correction, URGENT CNS NETWORK ADVISORY

(Eds: If you carried the entire CNS story regarding Hunter Tylo's $5 million jury award in the *Melrose Place* case, which ran Dec. 22, we would urge you to review the following and run a correction. The quotes from a law professor were near the end of the story.)

In a Dec. 22, 1997 story regarding a jury's award in the Hunter Tylo *Melrose Place* trial, CNS included quotes from a law professor which incorrectly characterized Spelling Entertainment attorney William Waldo's trial experience.

In fact, CNS has learned from Waldo that he is an employment lawyer who has extensive trial experience, has tried numerous jury trials in employment matters, and has developed and taught a course on jury trials in employment cases. He has recently obtained a defense verdict in a jury trial involving claims arising under the California Family Rights Act, and he is listed in "The Best Lawyers in America."

In addition, the CNS story quoting the law professor incorrectly characterized Waldo's basis of argument. In fact, Waldo has pointed out he did argue on the law of the contract in question on a number of occasions.

City News Service regrets these errors.
CNS-01-14-1998 13:00

All I could think: *What a bunch of pussies!*

I drove up to Century City at around 7:00 p.m. I was on edge and couldn't sit still. I didn't want to be high on coke when I saw Pat. I'd snorted my last line at 12:30 p.m. and my body desperately needed another bump. I started wondering how I would be able to continue to support my habit without a job.

I walked into Pat's office and he shook my hand. He was short, with silver hair, and didn't look me directly in the eyes when he spoke. "Let's go down to the bar and chat."

The high-rise that housed City News had a small bar on the ground floor. Pat and I sat in a booth. A waitress walked over and asked us what we wanted to order.

"Jack Daniels," I said. "On the rocks. In a tall glass."

"A Coke, please," Pat said.

Pat was stumbling on his words.

"You know Jason…let's see…where do I start…well, hmm… you've had hundreds of spelling and grammatical errors since you started here six months ago," he said, looking down at his glass of Coke. "We need someone who can self-edit. Plus, you don't write as much as your predecessor. And then there's the correction…"

"Yeah," I said, sneering at Pat, hoping I would scare the bejesus out of him with my *I'm going to kill you* stare.

"Well…I really hate this…I never liked this part of my job… we've decided not to extend your probationary period," he said. "You would be much better off working at a newspaper where you can get more attention and hand-holding."

I took a gulp of Jack Daniels. Pat opened up his briefcase, took out an envelope, and handed it to me.

"This is two weeks' severance," he said. "Hopefully, it will get you through while you look for another job."

"Gee, thanks," I said sarcastically. I knew there was no chance I could talk Pat out of firing me, not after he ran that extensive correction.

Pat put out his hand and said goodbye. I took another gulp of the Jack Daniels and shook his hand and squeezed real hard and tried to make eye contact, but he wouldn't have any of it.

I sat back down and ordered another Jack Daniels and tore open the envelope. Fifteen-hundred dollars—that was my severance. I imagined all of the coke I could buy with the money. I finished my drink and drove to the ATM machine where I deposited the severance check and took out 300 dollars, the maximum withdrawal allowed. I paged my dealer and met him at a grocery store on Laurel Canyon. He gave me a palm-sized rock of coke and I handed him fifteen twenty-dollar bills. I sat in my car, gently broke the rock in half, and chopped up the biggest lines on a plastic CD jewel case. I snorted half of the coke in less than ten minutes. As I drove home, I thought the FBI was following me.

I drove down some side streets in Beverly Hills, but I couldn't shake those headlights in my rearview mirror. The imaginary rats crawling up my leg made me crash my car into the curb. I put the car in park, got out, and pulled down my pants in the middle of the street, looking inside my underwear for rodents. I banged my driver's seat thinking it would scare them away. My pants were around my ankles. I got back into the car and cut another line on the CD case of the Rolling Stones album *Let It Bleed*. I hoped the coke would knock some reality into me. But the panic attacks started again.

I was drooling out of the side of my mouth. My speech was slurred. I ran into my house and snuck into the bathroom before I saw Lisa.

"Jason? Is that you?"

"Yeah, I'm going to the bathroom," I said.

"You don't even say hello first?" she said, annoyed.

In the bathroom, I ripped off my clothes and shook my underwear to see if any rats fell out. I did the same thing with my jeans. I couldn't face Lisa in that condition. I turned on the shower. Made it real cold and got in. The shock of the cold water knocked me out of my paranoid state of mind. I dried off and went downstairs to tell Lisa I got fired.

"What's going on with you?" she asked.

"What are you talking about?"

"You're acting really weird."

The next morning I got a call from a woman who said she was a lawyer representing City News. She told me that Spelling's attorney was not satisfied with the correction and he filed a lawsuit against me, City News, Stan Goldman, the Fox News pundit who gave me the quote, and the *Pasadena Star-News*. She said City News wanted to try and settle the matter immediately and all of the parties involved agreed to meet with an arbitrator to see if we could reach a settlement. She said she would be representing City News and me.

"Would you be willing to meet with the arbitrator?" she asked.

"Uh, yeah, I guess."

The next day I went the arbitrator's office. Doug Faigan, the president of City News, was there with the company's attorney, the woman I had spoken to on the phone. Doug tried to be nice but I gave him the cold shoulder because I was pissed off about being fired.

We went into a conference room, and sitting around a long, rectangular table were Goldman, his attorney, Spelling's attorney and his personal counsel, and an attorney for the *Star-News*. I sat down in one of the empty seats far away from all of the key players. The arbitrator explained that it would be in everyone's interest to settle the issue and avoid a costly legal battle.

"This is what I hope to achieve today," he said.

He asked Spelling's attorney to make an opening statement. I wanted to smash Spelling's attorney in the back of the head with a baseball bat. He said that my story made him the laughingstock of his law office and that he lost the respect of his friends and family.

"Maybe you lost everyone's respect because you lost the case, you fucking prick," I said to myself.

He said he had also lost some clients. Then he held up a prescription bottle and tried to get everyone's sympathy.

"You know what this is?" he said, displaying the bottle of pills. "It's nitroglycerin tablets. I've been using them ever since this story appeared in the newspaper. It's supposed to help stop me from having a heart attack."

"Oh just drop dead already, you piece of shit," I said to myself.

I still didn't understand what I did wrong so I asked City News' attorney to define libel for me.

In order to be defamatory, the statement must be untrue. If the statement is true or substantially true, then it is not defamatory, and the case is over.

In order for the plaintiff to prevail, the statement must have caused real and substantial harm to the person or business. The plaintiff must present evidence of the substantial harm done.

The plaintiff must also show that the defendant knew the statement was untrue but published or broadcast the statement despite that knowledge.

How could this fucking thin-skinned attorney win a libel case against City News? There was no way he could prove that I knew Goldman's quote about his experience was untrue.

The arbitrator asked us to break up into groups. He said we have two choices: we could offer Spelling's attorney some money for his "pain and suffering" or we could refuse to give him any money then we would have no choice but to go to trial. The arbitrator said he would ask Spelling's attorney how much money he wanted to end the legal wrangling. Then he would communicate that to us and we would start negotiating.

Spelling's attorney asked for a figure everyone turned down as too high. After eight hours of negotiating it looked like we were still too far apart on terms. We would have to settle this in court. City News' attorney told me I would have to testify and that other media outlets may scrutinize me because the case was a spin-off of the Hunter Tylo case.

"People would probably be interested in writing about this," she said.

Then it hit me. If I went to court everyone would find out about my felony. That would ruin me. My entire life would be an open book. I would never work in journalism again. I couldn't let that happen.

"Can I speak to you privately?" I asked the attorney representing City News.

"Sure," she said.

We ducked out of the small office and went inside a room containing a copy machine.

"You're representing me here also, right?" I asked.

"Yes," she said.

"That means that you have to abide by attorney/client privilege, right?" I asked.

"That's true," she said.

"Okay. I am a convicted felon. What are the chances if we went to trial that would come out?"

"What were you convicted of?" she asked.

"Grand theft," I said.

"That's a credibility issue. It would definitely come out in a trial. They would try and find out everything about you," she said.

"Fuck. I want to settle this case tonight. I don't want this to go to trial. Can we make Spelling's attorney an offer, please?" I asked.

"Yes. I'll advise Doug that we should settle. Thank you for telling this to me. I know it must have been hard for you," she said.

A couple of hours later, City News, the *Star-News*, and Goldman settled with Spelling's attorney. I kept my secret.

At home, my paranoia became worse. As Lisa sought comfort in friends and family, I started to find notes she had written to discuss with a therapist she planned on seeing. Lisa was still under the impression that my delusions were the result of a brain disorder.

How do I cope with Jason when he's having an attack? How can I not be exhausted, not angry, but show Jason I love [she drew a heart instead of writing out "love"] him without him feeling abandoned? Jason doesn't see or understand the effect of seeing him behave this way on me and what being sleep deprived and exhausted does to me. Anger: I knew life with him would not be easy, but I was not prepared for this. Passivity of Jason: to help himself why isn't he taking meds, going to an anxiety clinic? I can't do it for him. He needs to stand up. Jason thinks I don't love him. He was never taught that you could love someone and be furious with them too.

Lisa saw her therapist a day after I read her notes. She didn't discuss her session with me, but she suggested that she and I immediately attend a couples counseling session together. She left me a note.

Dear Jason:

I love you very much but I feel our relationship is in a very precarious time in our marriage. I want to work it out but I don't think either of us have the tools. The only way I feel we have a chance is if we go into couples counseling. At this point, it is the only thing I feel will help. I am truly at my breaking point and can't continue like this anymore. I'm sorry that by being honest with you that you doubt my love or think that I don't want to be married to you anymore. I can promise you that I have never stopped loving you.

Love,
Lisa

The couples counseling session would be the second time Lisa saved my life. It took five minutes for her therapist to figure out I was on drugs, and that it was the reason I was having panic attacks. He told Lisa to arrange an intervention. That's the day I hit bottom, July 10, 1998, and went into rehab. I've been sober ever since.

SIX

I'M SITTING INSIDE A conference room at the *Los Angeles Times* in Santa Monica filling out an employment application. The dreaded question stares me down: "Have you ever been convicted of a felony?" I start thinking about what I was taught at my first Alcoholics Anonymous meeting 120 days earlier, and hope it would help me to answer the question correctly.

God grant me the serenity to accept the things I cannot change, the courage to change the things I can, and the wisdom to know the difference.

I can't answer it truthfully, and respond to the question as if I'm offended by the query. I color in the "no" box with my black ballpoint pen until the tip of the pen tears through the paper. There's my answer. Happy? Then I lie about my education. I say I graduated from New York University with a bachelor's degree in journalism.

This was the umpteenth time in my life that I had to start from scratch and reinvent myself. I no longer could anesthetize my body with drugs and alcohol to ease the pain I felt from being alive. Lisa said she'd leave me if that ever happened again, and without her I'd surely die. I really did want to be a good person, and I believed that having a reporting job at the *Los Angeles Times* would make me one.

I thumb through the pile of newspaper clippings I've written since I moved to Los Angeles in June 1996. They're not bad. I'm qualified for the job. I can do this. I take the application and clips to Phil Bonney, the editorial recruiter, who sits outside the conference room waiting for me. And I become the person I pretend to be in my application.

"So, you graduated New York University?" Phil asks, perhaps suspiciously, or so I think.

"Uh, yeah. I majored in journalism. Graduated in '92."

"Hmm. There's a one-year gap in your resume. What were you doing between 1993 and 1994?"

The question floored me. I intentionally blocked bad years from my mind, and now there they were, filling my head during the interview, like seeing my parents for the first time after I got committed.

◇

I WAS SCARED AND nervous. I didn't want to look like a drug addict but I did, and Mom would be able to tell. I looked at my reflection in the bathroom mirror and even though I had regained some weight I didn't look the same any more. My long hair was gone, my eyes were droopy, and my skin white as a dove. The symptoms of my withdrawals were resurfacing. I was very shaky and could not stop my jaw from twitching.

I tried to find the right clothes to wear so I would look presentable when my parents arrived, but I didn't have any. Just my uniform throughout life—a T-shirt and jeans. I would have killed for a three-piece suit at that moment. I did my best to make the T-shirt look neat by tucking it into my jeans, but it kept coming undone. My waist was still too small to hold up my jeans. I lost seventy-three pounds snorting cocaine for over two years.

The therapist walked into the bathroom and said it was time. My mom and dad were waiting in her office. My palms were sweaty and my jaw continued to twitch. I couldn't stop rubbing my hands. We walked down the hallway for what seemed like an eternity and I thought about hundreds of different scenarios. I never imagined my life would end up like this. Patients were walking around in their bathrobes, muttering to themselves. Old men and women sat at a table making leather belts and drawing pictures with crayons. It reminded me of the time I was in kindergarten and drew pictures of the sun and of birds and clouds for my parents to hang on the refrigerator—which they never did.

My therapist took out a white plastic card from her pocket and rubbed it against a piece of metal until security doors opened. I looked behind me to make sure I wouldn't forget where I spent the summer of 1993.

Mom and Dad were sitting on a couch that had a view of the hospital courtyard. They could see all of the patients being supervised by a doctor who only let them outside to smoke cigarettes. Now my parents knew I was one of those crazy patients. Mom turned around first to look at me. It was the first time I had looked into my mother's eyes in four months. She was wearing a denim jacket with rhinestones on the sleeves and a picture of the New York skyline in glitter on the back. Her blonde hair smelled of Miss Breck hairspray, confirming that it really was my mother sitting there in front of me. My dad was still looking out the window. I was scared of him and prayed that he wouldn't acknowledge my presence.

Mom looked me over and let out a soft "hi." It sounded awkward, like she was meeting me for the first time. I nodded my head and said, "Hello." My mom, always the drama queen, started to weep. I didn't feel sorry for her. At that moment, I blamed her for everything. She's manipulative. She's a liar. When I was thirteen, I was digging through her purse looking for cigarettes and instead found a bag filled with pot and a pack of EZ-Wider rolling papers. I confronted her about it. She didn't bother asking what I was doing in her purse; instead she concocted this story about a co-worker who gave her the pot saying she could use it to spice up the tomato sauce she was cooking that night to pour over the spaghetti.

"Well, what about the rolling papers? What's that for?" I asked.

"My friend said I could use it to clean my eyeglasses," she said with a straight face. She was a good teacher when it came to lying.

I accused her of trying to get the whole family high and handed her the weed and the rolling papers, and when she wasn't looking I grabbed a handful of her pot for myself.

My mother's eye makeup was running down her cheeks. A drop landed on her blouse, leaving a black mark that looked like a bullet wound.

"Why, Jason? Why, Jason? Why are you trying to hurt me?"

All I could say was "I'm sorry," with no feeling attached to those two words. It was my mother I thought about every time I put my nose to the mirror and watched those thin white lines disappear. She allowed my father to beat me whenever I got into deep shit—the kind that resulted in a phone call from my friends' parents saying I stole money from their house, a report from the principal saying I ripped off money from other students' lockers during gym class, or a visit from a police officer to say he caught me trespassing on private property. I wanted her to feel the pain that stayed with me long after the bruises my father gave me had healed.

My father turned around to face me and I could see rage in his face. His hair was styled like Elvis Presley's and his full beard and the Panther tattoo emblazoned on his right bicep fit the stereotypical biker image that made people in our neighborhood fear him.

"You know, Jason, I would love to kick the shit out of you right now," my father said. "You're a good-for-nothing junkie. You ruined your whole life."

I started to cry. I wished I were strong enough to beat my father to death. At that moment, I wanted him to die slowly. I wanted to watch him suffer.

I was nineteen years old when I first plotted to murder my father. I was sitting at the kitchen table at our house with my younger sister, Michelle, her boyfriend Scott, a black belt in tae kwon do, and my father, also a black belt in tae kwon do. Michelle and my father were engaged in a hostile discussion about her future after high school. Michelle didn't want to go to college and told that to my father, who insisted that was where she was headed because he didn't work as hard as he did so she would wind up with no future. Scott and I sat there and watched, enjoying the confrontation.

Michelle said defiantly, "It's my life. I can do what I want."

"Don't you dare talk back to me. Don't...you...dare," my father said, his voice reaching a high pitch-a warning sign that he was about to take this argument to the next level.

"Don't point your finger at me," Michelle said, standing up to him with a set of balls I wished I had.

Michelle egged him on, daring him to do something about her defiance. Suddenly, with what seemed like the speed of Randy Johnson, my father pitched a heavy ceramic mug at Michelle's head. She put her arm across her face to block the mug and it shattered, breaking her wrist. She let out a horrific scream and fell to the floor writhing in pain. My father walked quickly out of the kitchen into his bedroom. I sat at the kitchen table for a couple of seconds with a hand over my mouth. Then I moved into action. I told Scott, who was on the floor trying to soothe my sister, to go into my father's bedroom and keep him there.

"Don't fucking let him leave," I said. "Block the door if you have to."

I couldn't look at Michelle, who was moaning. I started to cry, opened up the knife drawer, grabbed the biggest one, and then walked slowly towards my father's bedroom. But he was already gone. Scott said he had a feeling that I was going to do something I would regret and urged my father to leave the house immediately. I told Scott I wouldn't have any regrets. It would've been worth it.

Scott carried Michelle to his car and we drove her to the emergency room, where she told the doctor tending her wrist that she crashed her bicycle into a tree.

My father didn't return home for two days. I drank a couple of fifths of Jack Daniels those two nights and imagined slicing open my father's throat while he slept. I begged my mother to leave him, but she said that Michelle provoked him and that if we were "well-behaved children" my father wouldn't lose his temper. Michelle eventually forgave my father. I never did.

Back at the mental hospital, my father stared me down. My legs were shaking as I stood up and took a small step toward my father, leaned my head forward and said, "Fuck you." That's all I could do with the rage I felt in the pit of my stomach. He didn't say a word, just stared at me and cracked his knuckles. He probably would have pounded me if my therapist and a few security guards hadn't been in the room

My mother said she wanted me to come home. I had nowhere else to go and was penniless, so I agreed. I think my mother felt obligated to be a mother at that moment. It certainly wasn't out of love. At least it didn't feel that way to me.

I spent the rest of the year holed up in my bedroom at my parents' house and landed my first journalism job in January 1994, working as an editorial assistant at the *Reporter Dispatch* newspaper in White Plains.

I've always loved newspapers; I'd collected them as a kid. The smell of a paper after removing it from a bundle was delicious. I was such a newspaper nerd that I even wore T-shirts emblazoned with *The New York Times* logo. I was a paperboy and moved up to the customer service desk at the Bergen Record when I graduated high school.

When I got the job at the *Dispatch*, I was responsible for writing all the obituaries and religion briefs. I don't know why they hired me. I didn't even have a college degree. That was the first time I lied on my resume for a job. I worked at the paper for nearly a year, eventually moving back to Manhattan in December 1994 to look for a job with the music industry.

I COULDN'T HELP BUT lie to Phil at the *Los Angeles Times* interview when he asked me about what I did in 1993.

"Oh, right, 1993. I was actually helping my brother launch his home improvement business, but it didn't work out because I realized that I didn't enjoy manual labor."

Phil looked over my clips again, and explained what the reporting job was all about. It was far different from what I had expected.

The *Times* had a division called *Times Community News* that employed former *Times* freelancers and recent college graduates for 20,000 dollars a year. Also known as *TCN*, the community news division consisted of a half-dozen community newspapers that contained local news, human-interest stories, and high school sports scores. These newspapers, such as the *Westside Weekly*, *South Bay Weekly*, *Glendale News-Press*, and *Daily Pilot*, were inserted into regional editions of the *Los Angeles Times*. The Glendale edition of the *Los Angeles Times* also came with the *Glendale News-Press*, the Newport Beach edition came with a copy of the *Daily Pilot*, the community newspaper that covered Newport Beach.

The community newspapers looked more like advertising circulars than legitimate news publications. The goal of the community papers was to connect with the readers who believed the *Times* spent too much time trying to distinguish itself as a national newspaper at the expense of local news. By creating a community news division, the paper was able to continue to focus on its national and statewide news coverage without having to use its staffers to cover local issues. And because advertising in the community papers was brisk, they brought in steady revenue.

Instead of getting Staff Writer bylines like stories written for the main edition of the *Times*, the *TCN* reporters' bylines would read "Special to the Times" in order to separate the old-time staff writers from the ugly stepchildren. No one who worked as a *Times* freelancer liked this setup, but Los Angeles was pretty much a one-newspaper town and reporting jobs were hard to come by.

Phil told me that if I were to get the job I would be working in Costa Mesa for the Orange County edition of the *Times*, a hundred-mile round-trip commute from my Los Angeles apartment. He said that I would be required to write a thirty- to fifty-word brief about something I found newsworthy for the paper's scan page, a snapshot of what's happening in all of the cities in Orange County, much like *USA Today's* States page. Phil said there might be an opportunity to write bigger stories for the countywide edition of the newspaper once the editors got to know me and if I found something newsworthy on my beat. He said the job paid 450 dollars a week.

"I'm your man, Phil," I said. "This sounds like a great opportunity."

"Well, I do have other people to interview," he said. "But I like your clips. I'll send them over to the folks in the Orange County office to get their input and I'll get back to you."

I would have taken that job if it only paid a dollar. In my situation—fresh out of rehab, one year into a five-year probation sentence—being picky wasn't an option. After saying goodbye to Phil, I walked across the street to the Santa Monica Courthouse to meet with my probation officer. I lived a double life. On the outside, I was always smiling and trying to make people laugh, and on the inside I had no idea how to be myself. Afraid of being judged and rejected, I made up stories about my past, my education, and my job experience, hoping to fit in. I always worried that someone would discover my secrets and expose me. Yet I also went out of my way to get attention. Working as a reporter and seeing my name in print was like daring someone to rip off my disguise. I have to admit I did get a rush out of the scam.

My marriage was barely hanging together. Lisa still didn't trust me and I couldn't blame her. I spent a year snorting coke and drinking behind her back. I couldn't understand why she stayed with me.

Sometimes, I'd sneak into our bedroom and watch Lisa sleep and wonder to myself how I could have caused her so much pain. When her eyes are shut and she's wrapped in a blanket nobody looks more innocent. I just want to crawl up next to her and cradle her in my arms. I keep the image of Lisa lying peacefully in the front of my mind to ward off the urge to start drinking and drugging again.

"I know what you're capable of. I believe in you," Lisa said. I needed constant affirmation from her. But I couldn't get too close to her physically. No kissing. She wasn't ready for that yet. I told Lisa that the interview went well and she crossed her fingers, wiped her mouth, and walked to the kitchen to prepare dinner. I didn't want to lose her. Everyone I met at A.A. meetings told me I had to stay sober for me, but I was really doing it because I didn't want to lose Lisa.

Phil called me a week later to offer me the job. He said my clips—one on a murder trial, one on a celebrity who successfully sued producer Aaron Spelling, and a feature story on a woman who had been a foster mother to 300 children—stood out from the other candidates he interviewed.

"Are you serious?" I said loudly into the phone. "Phil, thank you so much. You've made me so happy. I hope I can repay you one day."

"Just do a good job. That'll make me look good," Phil said.

"Count on it, Phil," I replied.

"Oh, I forgot," Phil said. "You'll need to take a drug test. Do you have a problem with that?"

"Absolutely not," I said. "Bring it on."

I've been sober four months, I thought, *long enough for my body to rid itself of the evidence.*

I peed into the plastic cup proudly, as if I'd get an extra gold star for all my drug-free urine. I walk to my car confident this is the first test I will get a perfect score on. No one at the *Los Angeles Times* will ever know that I've spent my twenties using cocaine and plenty of other illegal drugs. I worry, though, that someone at the newspaper will do a background check.

"A felony? Me? You're kidding?" I say to myself stuck in freeway traffic, imagining someone from the *Times* is confronting me with my past. "Are you sure you got the right Jason Leopold? I've never been arrested before. This must be a mistake."

I arrived at the *Los Angeles Times*' Orange County edition on a Monday morning dressed in khakis, a blue shirt, and a gray, patterned tie. My shoes were so perfectly polished you'd think I spent time in boot camp.

The newsroom at the *Times* was enormous and cold, like a morgue. I'd never been in a newsroom that big before, but it was exactly like I had imagined, smelling of lousy coffee and stale air. A tall, gangly guy in thick-framed glasses was shouting across the newsroom to a reporter, "You file that story yet?" Reporters and editors balanced their telephone receivers between their shoulders and ears and violently tapped their computer keyboards— clickety clickety clack—and the phones kept ringing-ding-a-ling, ding-a-ling, ding-a-ling. It sounded like a symphony and it gave me goosebumps. Old, yellowing newspapers were stacked on the floor. Documents and notebooks were strewn across every desk, like an inner-city hospital emergency room. There was no time for order. Every story was treated as if it meant the difference between life and death.

I blanked out everything Phil Bonney told me about the job and was already focusing on my first assignment, hoping it would be a shooting or a bank robbery. I spent a year covering stories like that at the two other news organizations I worked for in Los Angeles, but they were small-time operations.

Jill Jones—pretty, blonde, and plump—was my boss. She told me that I would be given the Laguna Beach beat, spending most of my time writing briefs. The only thing I knew about Laguna Beach is that it was where Lisa and I had our first date two years earlier, at a restaurant called Five Feet—ironic because that's Lisa's exact height. Laguna Beach was one of two liberal cities (because it had a gay community) in Republican-dominated Orange County. People who lived in my neck of the woods, Los Angeles' Westside, would travel to Laguna Beach for a quick weekend getaway. Now I would have to drive sixty-five miles every day just to bring back a thirty-word brief to Jill so she could include it in the *Times'* scan page. Here's an example of what I wrote for the *Times* during my first four months on the job.

> The Laguna Beach City Council will meet Tuesday to consider architectural designs for the city's new $25 million resort hotel, which is expected to open for business in the summer of 2002. The meeting starts at 7:00 p.m. in council chambers.

The *Times* had a staff of seven reporters who did this kind of shit every day, for which they were paid the grand sum of twenty grand a year.

I was given a desk at the back of the newsroom, near the exit, where all the other community news reporters were isolated. The *Times* brass made it a point to separate us from them. On the one hand, the editors hated us because we were hacks who reputedly scummed up the pristine *Times*. On the other hand, they needed us because the paper couldn't get anyone else to file those stupid briefs, the bread and butter of the newspaper. Surveys showed that more people read the scan page than any other part of the newspaper.

I didn't mind sitting at the back of the newsroom as it made it easy for quick cigarette escapes, which, much to my surprise, was a habit I did not share with other newsroom reporters. There was no old-time glamour here. No chain-smokers, no drunken reporters phoning in stories from the local watering hole, and no sign of liquor bottles stashed in desk drawers.

I spent the first month at the *Times* listening to my young colleagues complain about their lowly positions because they studied journalism at the best colleges. They all thought they deserved the best assignments despite the fact that they were greener than moldy bread. None of them, however, asked the editors if they could go out and cover a story. Journalism is about aggressiveness, passion, truth, and most importantly, asking questions. If you can't even get off your ass and ask an editor to put you on a story, how is that editor supposed to send you out to ask strangers questions?

Every other Tuesday the Laguna Beach City Council meets, and it was my job to monitor that exciting event for potential news. City Hall, where the council meets, was one block from the beach. I spent the first thirty minutes of the meeting watching the waves because that's when the council takes attendance and reads minutes of the previous meeting into the record. I then walk back to City Hall, drop a quarter in a homeless guy's cup, and take a seat on a metal folding chair. I know the three-hour meeting is about to end when my ass falls asleep.

"Okay, we've got a lot of ground to cover tonight so let's get right to it," a council member says. I'm doodling in my reporter's notebook and can't see the person behind the high-pitched male voice. "We have an application here from a Chris Spencer of Spencer Recovery Center, a sober living facility. Mr. Spencer, are you here?"

I immediately lift my head and look around the room for this Spencer. The words "sober living" pique my interest; it's a place where serious drug addicts and alcoholics go after rehab because they still can't be trusted. Sober living (a house in a residential neighborhood where sobering addicts live for six months) is supposed to keep the addict away from drugs and alcohol and teaches them how to live a drug-free life.

Chris Spencer breezes by me. His face is worn, like an old leather shoe, and his suit smells musty, like it's been in a closet for a couple of years. He's got a thick moustache and his hair is parted in the middle. He looks like he abused drugs for a long time.

"Chris Spencer. Right here, sir," he says as he makes his way up to the podium to talk to the council.

"Mr. Spencer," says a council member. "You're asking the council to approve your application to turn your sober living facility into some type of medical detoxification hospital? Can you explain what you mean?"

"Gladly. What I want is to offer twenty-four hour emergency medical care to people who are just getting off drugs or alcohol. I want this to also be a place where they can come and detox. I plan to administer medicine to help with the withdrawals."

I know exactly what Spencer is talking about. The first three days after you stop using drugs or alcohol are like being sentenced to purgatory. Your body shakes uncontrollably, you can't sleep, and all you want is more drugs or alcohol to stop the physical pain. During my first week in rehab the doctors prescribed a shitload of medicine that made me sleep off the worst part of detox.

"Mr. Spencer, your facility is located in a residential area," the council member says. "We can't allow you to perform this type of service because of city ordinances. We can't have ambulances and cars traveling in your area all hours of the night disturbing the other residents. I'm sorry but we're going to have to turn down your request."

"But I've already been doing it for about a year," Spencer says. "I don't see what the fuss is all about."

Ding-ding-ding-ding-ding-ding-ding. Jackpot. Like a dog sniffing for food, I begin to smell a story. It's instinctive, my ability to sense a news story. You just know when it happens, sort of like falling in love. This wasn't just any story; it was my first story for the *Los Angeles Times*. I scribble the exchange between Spencer and the councilman sitting on the edge of my chair. I wait to see how the rest of the saga unfolds. The four other council members are stunned by Spencer's admission.

"Are you telling this council that you've been using your sober living facility as a hospital, in defiance of the city's ordinance?" the council member asks loudly.

"I'm licensed by the state to treat people in the initial stages of recovery," Spencer says, in his own defense. "So I figured it's okay."

The council lashes back at Spencer, explaining that the permit he got from the city says that his sober living house can only be used to give addicts a place to sleep after they have spent at least a month in another recovery center. The council also tells Spencer that city zoning laws supersede his state license. They demand that he stop detoxing addicts and threaten to shut him down if he doesn't.

I head to the pay phone outside of City Hall. It's about 8:30 p.m. and if I get this story to Jill by 9:00 p.m. it could make the morning paper. I call Jill and tell her what happened at the council meeting—and she's not impressed.

"Well, I suppose if we don't cover it we'll look stupid," she says. "I can give you ten inches of column space. That's about 300 words."

Jill tells me to write the story by hand and phone it in to her. I'm nervous because I really want to impress her, but I'm also scared because I only have three minutes to write it and I'm not sure if I can pull it off. I fumble with the lede.

"A Laguna Beach man admitted Tuesday that he…" I write in my notebook. No, that sounds stupid. I tap into my memory of the one journalism class I took in college, recalling what my professor said: "What's the news? Make believe you're telling this to your mother, then write it that way."

Laguna Beach officials said Wednesday that they will require the owner of a beachfront drug and alcohol recovery center to stop offering medical detoxification there.

Christopher C. Spencer, owner of Spencer Recovery Center at 1316 S. Coast Highway, admitted violating the permit he received in March 1997 to open his center. But he said that his institution is licensed by the state to give medical assistance to drug addicts and alcoholics in the initial stage of recovery and that he was unaware he had to meet separate city standards.

I phone Jill back and read her the story. She makes a few edits, thanks me, and hangs up. My confidence rises. I feel legitimate.

The next day, I get to the *Times* office an hour early because I want to see the story on newsprint. I want to see my byline in capital letters. I grab four papers from the stack by the city desk. The papers are fresh. You can still smell the ink. I head over to my desk and pull out the Metro section from the middle of the newspaper and start scanning the paper. There's the story, buried deep within the Metro section on page B4. I just stare at my byline like a proud parent.

BY JASON LEOPOLD
SPECIAL TO THE TIMES

I didn't understand why everyone complained about the "Special to the Times" line. I thought it sounded sophisticated. It made me feel like I was a special correspondent working undercover in some far-off land.

The editors chipped away at excess fat in my story—cutting a verb, an adjective, moving up compelling quotes—and after reading it I couldn't believe it was mine. It looked so professional that I felt I should be wearing a uniform that said "professional journalist."

The city editor of the *Times* walks over to my desk. It's the first time I've met him since I started at the paper a month ago.

"Good work on that story last night," says the city editor, patting me on the back. "We beat the *Register*. Mind doing a follow-up today?"

The *Orange County Register* is the other county newspaper, and the competition between the *Times* and the *Register* was fierce. The *Register*'s circulation surpasses the *Times*' by about 100,000 copies. The *Register* has a conservative agenda, while the *Times* tends toward liberalism. There were rumors that *Register* reporters and *Times* reporters got into brawls at press conferences over access to sources. If a story appears in the *Times* that isn't in the *Register* the same day, the reporter on that beat gets a phone call from a *Register* editor early in the morning demanding to know why.

"Absolutely," I say to the city editor. "I'll follow up the story right now."

The other reporters I sat next to were resentful because I had worked at the paper for a shorter period of time than they had, and I already had a byline. Since I wasn't interested in becoming friendly with any of them I alienated them from my life. They were unpopular with the staff at the *Times* because they were so green.

I wrote a follow-up story after getting comments from leather-faced Spencer and members of the city council. The *Times* ran it in the paper the next day on page B5. The *Register* printed its own version, lagging a day behind mine.

Jill feeds my ego with compliments about the Chris Spencer story and asks me if I would be interested in working a Sunday shift to cover for a reporter on vacation. She explains that none of the staff reporters like to work Sundays and it could be a good opportunity for me to get some more clips. She says I would be the only reporter working and I would have to cover breaking news in addition to one assignment.

"I think you could handle it based on your performance reporting these last two stories," she says.

"I would love to do that," I respond. "Thank you for thinking of me."

I'm starting to believe all of the clichés I hear at A.A. meetings. "If you live a life clean and sober good things will come your way." I don't bother telling the other reporters about my latest coup. I step outside to phone Lisa to tell her how well I'm doing. "I'm so proud of you," she says. "Stay with it."

I get to the *Times* at about 9:00 a.m. that Sunday. My first assignment: humpback whales are spotted in Huntington Beach, a rarity, apparently. I drive out to meet with a marine biologist. I see a whale but so damn what. I speak to a few residents and drive back to file the story, and then phone all of the police stations in the county to see if there is any breaking news. I'm told about a guy who is ejected from a car and killed during a police chase. Another cop tells me about a bunch of preppy kids who vandalized a few public schools in the middle of the night causing about 100,000 dollars in damage. I write them up. My adrenaline is pumping. It's 7:00 p.m., and now I'm working overtime. The photo editor at the paper gives me a tip about a twenty-year-old budding rock star and black belt in tae kwon do who is killed by a kick to the head during a martial arts competition.

"Oh shit!" I say to myself. Tae kwon do. I was afraid that irony would drop in on me again.

My father, a fourth-degree black belt in tae kwon do, sometimes travels around the country as a referee for tournaments. I become convinced that my father was the ref when this kid keeled over. It's been two years since I stopped speaking to my parents. The memories of the childhood beatings continue to haunt me.

I talk to the police investigator on the tae kwon do scene, the paramedic, and the man in charge of the competition. The paramedic says a blood vessel in the kid's head burst, but they're going to do an autopsy to determine the cause of death. I run out of the convention center because I'm afraid that the sight of him would trigger a fatal drug binge.

I was again being paranoid. My father wasn't there. Maybe deep down I was hoping I could see him. I wonder how he's aged over the past two years. I wonder if he's thinking about me.

I type up the story about that kicked-in-the-head kid, putting my total for the day at four news stories. It's 9:00 p.m. I'm exhausted, but still thinking about my father.

Everyone stares at me when I walk into the *Times* newsroom Monday morning. My guilty conscience convinces me I must have done something wrong. Did I fuck up one of the stories? Did I get a fact wrong? Did they find out about my felony? I slyly move my hand toward my pants. My zipper's zipped. Just then everyone in the newsroom starts applauding.

"You kicked ass yesterday!" one reporter says to me. "Good job," says another.

"Three bylines. I would have been more impressed with four," an editor says to me sarcastically.

"You beat the *Register* on two stories. They didn't have the tae kwon do story," Jill says.

I can still feel the handprints on my back when I unfold Monday's *Times*. On the front page I see my name. There are six news stories on the front page of Metro. My name appears twice there, once more inside. (The fourth story, one about a humpback whale, would run the following day.)

"Holy fucking shit," I whisper to myself. "One, two, three… Oh…my…God"

Jill tells me she can't remember the last time a reporter had three consecutive bylines in the paper, let alone two on the front page of the Metro section.

I collect about fifteen copies of the Metro section as souvenirs. I go outside to smoke a cigarette. I take a deep drag and exhale. I feel like a fraud. I don't deserve these accolades. I don't have a college degree and I'm a convicted felon. I have to report to a probation officer. Good things are not supposed to happen to people like me. I can't understand why I'm being given another chance. I feel like I'm living a lie. These people don't know anything about me.

Jill sends me an e-mail saying she wants to meet with me about a new project the *Times* is undertaking to boost the Orange County edition's circulation. It's top secret, she says.

Jill and I walk together toward the paper's conference room not saying a word to each other along the way. She explains the project, sounding like a saleswoman in a clothing store.

"We're going to launch a zoned edition of the *Times* in Laguna Beach," she said. "The Metro section will have three pages of local news. We're calling it *Our Times*."

"You mean those horrible inserts like they have in L.A.?" I ask.

"No. Here's the difference. The *Our Times* section will actually be part of the Metro section. It won't be a stand-alone insert. A full column on the left front will have community news from Laguna Beach five times a week and there will be two pages inside Metro for other news and features and a page for high-school sports," Jill said. "We're hoping to attract more subscribers by showing them that we'll be covering their neighborhood."

"What do you want me to do?"

"We need someone aggressive who can go out and dig for news and the editors here picked you," she says. "You were actually hand-picked for the job."

I'm not flattered by the proposal. *Our Times* has a terrible reputation. Mark Willes, the former chairman of cereal maker General Mills, became the publisher of the *Times* a few years back (he's known around the *Times* as the "Cereal Killer") and came up with this plan to increase the circulation of the *Times* by one million copies. Launching *Our Times* was one way Willes hoped to accomplish that goal.

The Metro reporters, however, are inexperienced, the editors can't edit, and the product design makes college newspapers look like *The New York Times*. I don't want to do it. I want to be a staff writer for the *Times*.

"You'll get that chance," Jill says. "Especially if you help produce news for this new section."

"Can I think about it?" I ask.

"Of course," she said. "Oh, I neglected to tell you that if you do decide to do it you'll have to move out of this office and work out of the *Daily Pilot* in Newport Beach. That's where Metro is going to be produced."

I want to please Jill but this job seems like a step down. Now I would have to tell people that I'm a reporter for *Our Times*, a second-rate news operation.

Why do I always worry about what other people think? I measure success on where I work and live and the car I drive. I'm already judging this new assignment even though Jill told me I was hand-picked for the job. A couple of months earlier I was unemployed and desperate.

I can't make the decision on my own. I discuss it with Lisa.

"Jason, this sounds like an amazing opportunity," she says. "Look how far you've come in just two months. Think of how much you can accomplish."

My conspiracy-theorist mind tells me that they offered the job to other reporters who turned it down. So I'm their last, easily manipulated hope.

My father once told me how he had an opportunity to buy into a fledgling business in the early '70s but decided not to. He stuck to driving a New York City cab because he had kids and was concerned that if the business failed he wouldn't be able to take care of his family.

"That company is now worth about twenty million dollars and I'm still driving a taxi," my father said years later. "Trust me, you don't want to go through life saying what if I did this or what if I did that. You'll always regret it."

That's the only piece of advice my father gave me that I followed.

SEVEN

"Jill, I'll take the job, but only on one condition," I said.

"Great news, Jason," Jill said. "What is it?"

"I would like to get paid an additional fifty dollars a week"

I could have asked for more but was afraid Jill would say no. I've never felt comfortable asking for money or toys or clothes or any of the stuff that kids usually beg their parents for. That's why I stole a librarian's credit card when I was in eighth grade. I figured I could just get what I wanted and wouldn't have to deal with my parents saying no.

"I can almost guarantee that it won't be an issue," Jill said, relieved, perhaps, that I didn't ask for more.

Bill Lobdell was the man in charge of *Times Community News* and the *Our Times* project. Technically, he was already my boss, even though we had never met. Bill was waiting for me in a *Times* conference room and Jill escorted me over to meet him. He stood up and shook my hand with a strong grip.

"I've heard a lot of great things about you," Bill said, sounding somewhat like a Valley girl. From the tone of his voice I assumed he was gay, but I later came to know he was straight. He was about six-foot-three, skinny, with high cheekbones, straight nose, and perfect teeth. He stood out among the editors and reporters who tended to have weight problems and pimples.

"It's a pleasure to meet you," I responded. "Thank you for the kind words."

Bill explained to me how *Our Times* was going to revolutionize the *Los Angeles Times* and force other mainstream newspapers in the country to adopt this type of business model. The *Times* launched *Our Times* in Santa Monica, where it ran three times a week. It filled the void in local news coverage when the *Santa Monica Outlook*, a paper that was around for more than one hundred years, shut down in 1997. *Our Times Santa Monica* was reputedly successful and one of the reporters there got a full-time staff position with the main edition of the *Los Angeles Times*.

"What do you mean by business model?" I asked.

"Let's face it, Jason, journalism is a business. It's about selling as many newspapers as you can and sometimes you have to come up with new ideas to do that. Don't get me wrong. *Our Times* is going to be a serious news operation. What I want you to do, what your job is, is to prove that news exists in these communities. Our expertise here at *TCN* is community news. That's what you need to concentrate on. My job is to make money for this company. *Our Times*, my baby, is going to do that and if our competitors are going to continue to compete with us they're going to have to conform," Bill said.

"I don't mean to sound negative, but are you saying that you think that adding a couple of pages of community news to the paper is going to get more people to subscribe?" I asked, sounding doubtful.

"Jason, the number one complaint that readers have with the *Times* is that it doesn't cover news about their neighborhood.

We did a survey and people said they would subscribe to the paper if it had more local news. So that's what we're going to give them," Bill said. "Think about it. We're making a dramatic editorial change to the *Times* by adding *Our Times*. That's never been done before and you are going to help us launch it. This is one of the most important jobs you'll ever have."

Bill made me feel like I should have been paying him for the job. He said he envisioned the L.A. edition of *Our Times* being broken up into two-dozen zoned editions, such as West Hollywood, Beverly Hills, Studio City, and so forth.

"Sounds like I found the place where I'll be working for a long time," I said to Bill.

"Glad to hear that," he said. "Why don't you come to the *Pilot* office on Tuesday and start then. Leslie, she's a *Pilot* editor, is going to be your editor and an editor. We launch in a month. This is a secret so don't discuss it with anyone here. Eventually, we plan to move all of the reporters working for the main paper to *Our Times*. "

I went back to my desk and told the other reporters that I would be moving out of the newsroom to go work on a special project for the *Times*. Apparently, the secret wasn't well kept in the newsroom.

"Are you going to work for *Our Times*?" one of the other reporters asked me.

"Shit, yeah, I am," I said. "But I'm not supposed to tell anyone about it."

"*Our Times* sucks," the other reporter said. "I can't believe you're going over. It's such a dumb idea. There's already a local section. It's called Metro."

The reporter tapped into my insecurity. I interpreted his comments as meaning that I was dumb, I sucked, I was stupid.

"You guys know as well as I do that Metro doesn't cover the whole county. Plus, you guys are eventually going to have to work for *Our Times*, too."

Our conversation attracted six other *TCN* reporters, who surrounded me, hoping to get the inside scoop on *Our Times*.

"What do you mean?" another reporter asked. "I ain't going to *Our Times*. I'm staying here."

"Lobdell said that eventually everyone here is going to become *Our Times* reporters," I said. "But you didn't hear that from me."

"Fuck that," steamed most of the reporters.

"I'll quit," said a female reporter.

"Look, Bill said *Our Times* is going to be a serious news operation. He said they're going to print *Our Times* in the Metro section. It's not going to be a stand-alone insert like L.A."

"Yeah, but the stories won't run in all of the editions of the *Los Angeles Times*. It will only be seen by people living in Ana-fucking-heim or fucking Laguna Beach," one of the reporters said.

"You guys are totally depressing me. I'm giving this a shot. The way I see it is a good reporter is a good reporter no matter where you work," I said, hoping this declaration would cure me of insecurity and self-doubt.

Truth is, I'm a victim of advertising. When Bill told me that we were going to change the face of journalism, I believed him.

I had been working at the *Times* for a little more than two months and had already made an impression on the senior editors. I wasn't sure if it was luck, being at the right place at the right time, or that a guardian angel was looking out for me. Just six months earlier I was in rehab, and close to death. Now I was going to help launch a new edition of the *Times*.

It took me nearly two hours to get to the *Daily Pilot* Tuesday morning. Lisa had bought me a ten-disc compact disc changer for my car to make the ride easier. It didn't help that day. My car was in the same spot for twenty minutes before traffic finally started to move. Then it stopped dead again. I rolled up the windows and screamed "FUUUUUUCK." I was certain that a conspiracy caused this traffic jam so I would be late for my first day of work on the new assignment.

If it weren't for the newspaper racks lined up against the wall you could easily mistake the *Daily Pilot* newsroom for a day-care center. It was about 1,500 square feet, with desks that looked as if they were donated by a city college. The depressing look of the thing made me think that the new job was a step down. The newsroom was packed with fifteen budding reporters—girls, lots of them—who were busy tossing mini-basketballs across the room and giggling about God-knows-what.

Bill had a small office against the wall where he could see everything going on in the newsroom. He was on the telephone when he spotted me, he quickly hung up and sprinted over to greet me.

"Hey! Jason! Welcome to the *Daily Pilot*. Let me give you a tour."

"Right here in the middle is where our six *Pilot* reporters work. That's Jennifer, that's Greg, there's Jessica, that's Kerry, my assistant. Behind these guys is where the copy editors sit. That's Sherman, Mike, Tony, and Steve. Over here in the corner is the photo department. This is Mark; he's in charge of the photo department. These are the designers. They design the *Pilot* and they'll be designing *Our Times*. That's Nancy, that's Joli, and that's Mary Beth. Oh, let me introduce you to Leslie, your new editor."

Everyone was extremely friendly and seemed genuinely interested in meeting me.

"Jason, this is Leslie, your editor at *Our Times*," Bill said, pushing me closer toward her.

"Hi, Leslie, nice to meet you," I said, sticking out my hand.

"Likewise. Bill has told me so many great things about you and I've seen your byline in the *Times*. Nice work," Leslie said and shook my hand.

"Okay. I'm going to leave you two alone to talk about coverage. Jason, this'll be your desk for now. Sorry it's so small," apologized Bill as he walked away. My desk was so close to Leslie's it seemed like we were sleeping together.

Leslie seemed way too young, too attractive, and too innocent to be an editor. She wore tight jeans and baggy shirts. I wondered how well a young thing like her could fine-tune one of my news stories.

"I started out as a reporter for the *Daily Pilot* two years ago and then got promoted to editor a year later, and now I'm an editor for *Our Times*," said Leslie.

"What did you do before the *Pilot*?" I asked.

"Nothing. The *Pilot* was my first job. I was in school before that," she said.

I was envious. I wanted Leslie's job. I didn't feel comfortable having her boss me around, but I kept my mouth shut and started working on finding stories in Laguna Beach. I had two weeks to find and write eight stories for a test run of the new section.

Finding newsy stories in Laguna Beach on a daily basis was a challenge. The small beach town didn't give me much to work with. The community news reporter has to look under rocks to find anything of interest. Sometimes I spent eight hours talking to people before I finally found enough to write about.

After educating me on the history of Laguna Beach, a librarian told me, "I can't say that anything interesting ever happens here, unless you think that someone who can't use their arms and paints using their nose is interesting. I mean, this woman has pieces hanging in the Museum of Modern Art."

The news I gathered during my first two weeks affected only a few blocks of people, not an entire city. The stories usually involved disputes between neighbors, such as one about a local resident who refused to follow a city ordinance to trim his trees.

Bill said the goal before we launched *Our Times* was for me to find a dozen or so "evergreen" stories—a news term that means articles that could run any time, to put in the bank, so to speak—so I could go out and spend more time getting to know people in the community and not have to worry about finding a story that day to write.

Leslie hired an editorial assistant to compile the calendar—a listing of events, such as art shows and readings, and the police blotter. She also hired a guy to cover high school sports. It turned out that three pages was a lot of space for just one town and we had a hard time plugging the holes in the page. So Bill came up with an idea.

"We're going to run the school lunch menu," he said proudly, like the father of a newborn baby.

I didn't say a word. I didn't even know how to respond. What would people think of me if I wrote for a section of the paper that said, "Tuesday's special: meatloaf with buttered peas and a fruit cup." I was already thinking about applying for a job elsewhere.

I left a message for the managing editor at the *Long Beach Press-Telegram*, the third largest newspaper in Southern California. It has a circulation of about 110,000 and is one of the *Times'* competitors.

The managing editor of the *Press-Telegram* agreed to interview me. I told Leslie I had a doctor's appointment and would be late for work. I met with the *Press-Telegram's* managing editor and divulged all of the secret details of the *Times' Our Times* project.

"Sheez. This is big news. Do you mind if I tell our editor-in-chief?" she asked.

"Not at all," I said. "But you didn't hear it from me."

"I suppose we'll need to figure something out to compete with *Our Times*," she said. "Listen, I'll look over your clips and keep them on file, but, unfortunately, we don't have anything available right now. That's supposed to change in about a month when one of our reporters goes on maternity leave. Between me and you I don't think she's coming back."

"Well, do keep me in mind."

I did, though, like the people I worked with at the *Pilot*. The reporters, copy editors, and designers were true individuals. It was like someone collected all the outcasts from high schools across America and dumped them in one small office. Some had multiple piercings; others had tattoos and blue hair. In time I felt like I belonged there.

We were two days away from launching *Our Times*. I had to give Leslie a list of stories I would be running, and then she would have to discuss those stories with Jill at the *Times* to make sure there was no overlap with the main paper. I couldn't imagine that anyone at the *Times* would be writing about a new local children's park or how residents complained about cellular phone antennas blocking their view of the beach. That's what I was reporting. One-paragraph stories that I had to pad out to ten huge paragraphs so the whole stinking page could be filled. When ad reps sold an extra page of ads, we were stuck with filling another page with text of some sort. I began to appreciate the daily lunch menus. When we ran out of copy, we'd run an entire month of them.

Our Times had to be the worst looking piece of newsprint I ever laid eyes on; it looked like a high school class project. As soon as I read the hard copy of a story I wrote, I knew I had to quit.

"WHO MASSACRED MY STORY?" I yelled across the *Pilot* newsroom.

Leslie ran over and grabbed the paper out of my hand, "What happened?"

"My story is filled with spelling errors. Someone performed surgery on it and never put it back together right."

Leslie brought up the story on her computer screen to check on the last copy editor.

"Fucking Sherman," Leslie said.

I followed Leslie to Sherman's desk.

"Sherman, can you explain what happened to Jason's story?" she asked. "It didn't look like this before we sent it over to you for a copy edit."

Sherman, a six-foot-two former football player with enormous biceps, stood up, picked the paper out of Leslie's hands with his thumb and index finger, and gave it a glance. He'd been working as a copy editor at *Pilot* for about five years.

"Looks okay to me," he said.

"Sherman, there are names spelled wrong and quotes that were deleted," Leslie responded.

"Well, you know what, I was overloaded with work yesterday. I had to edit five papers. This one got past me."

"Okay, I understand," Leslie said, walking back to her desk.

I didn't have the balls to say anything to Sherman. But I couldn't believe that you could get away with making these types of mistakes at a newspaper and not be held accountable. I told Leslie I needed to talk to her privately.

We went into the conference room where the entire office could see us through the glass windows.

"Listen, I'm sorry. I can't work here anymore," I said. "This is not turning out the way I thought it would."

Leslie made me feel like I was breaking up with her when she started to cry and then wobbled into Bill's office.

Ten minutes later, Leslie emerged from Bill's room, and a couple of girls went over to console her as she grabbed her purse and left.

I was still sitting in the conference room, scared to walk out, thinking I would be blamed for making Leslie cry. Bill came in and sat down next to me.

"Is Leslie all right?" I asked Bill.

"I told her to go home for the rest of the day," he said. "Leslie is a small-town girl and very sensitive. She told me that you want to quit. I can't let you do that. You're too valuable."

"I appreciate that, Bill, but I'm pissed off about my story being slaughtered, and frankly I think this job is better suited for someone just starting out."

"You also have to understand that there are going to be some road bumps along the way," Bill said. "I can't have you just throw in the towel before giving it a shot."

"I think I gave it a shot," I said.

"I've got an idea. We're going to be launching six editions of *Our Times* in the next three months. I just got the word. We're going to need to hire city editors and I think you would make a good city editor. What do you think?" Bill said.

"That sounds great," I said. "But I've never edited before."

"You'll learn as you go along," Bill said. "We don't even have reporters lined up for this yet. We've gotta launch in three months 'cause we need to increase circulation before the next audit. Most of the reporters we're going to hire will be very green because we can't offer them more than 20,000 dollars a year. I'll need you to show 'em the ropes."

"Well, do I get...you know...is there..."

"You'll get a ten thousand dollar raise," Bill said. "Your salary will be thirty-six thousand a year."

"I'll do it," I said.

Even though I agreed to take the city editor job, I didn't think I was cut out for it. I decided to call Jill. She'd have an honest opinion.

"Jason, sometimes good reporters don't make good editors," she said.

That wasn't the type of feedback I wanted to hear. So I went against her advice, deciding that I'd do the job and prove her wrong.

In four months, I went from being a lowly reporter to becoming a city editor. My edition of *Our Times* would be responsible for covering community news in Fullerton and Brea. That was somewhat of a relief because Fullerton is not without its news. It's got an airport, a college campus, a downtown district, and some crime, so I figured it shouldn't be terribly difficult to fill the pages. Brea, on the other hand, was a dead city, but it did have an occasional gang shooting.

Leslie returned to work the following day and apologized for her breakdown. I worked with her for two more weeks, writing stories about the town library and its collection of first-edition novels, the city's annual art show, and a local hairdresser. Bill said that circulation in Laguna Beach was up by about 900 subscriptions, but I doubted it. Every time I made a phone call to a city official or met someone in the street, I identified myself as an *Our Times* reporter and they seemed confused.

"Our who?" some people would say to me. "What's that?"

Bill said the *Times* was on the fast track to get fifteen *Our Times* editions out by the beginning of May.

"All we need are bodies," Bill said, referring to the reporters that he hoped to hire to fill the vacancies. "As long as they have a pulse and a heartbeat. That's all that matters now."

Most of the other reporters I worked with at the *Times* office in Costa Mesa had quit and found jobs at other newspapers because they didn't want to work for *Our Times*.

Management didn't seem to care about the quality of *Our Times*. They were too wrapped up in how much advertising space we sold, and they wanted to roll out new editions of the section quickly enough to please their bosses—the executives at the *Times* headquarters in Los Angeles.

A week later, Bill said he hired twelve reporters at a job seminar in Los Angeles. I became animated and cocky when those not very bright twelve reporters arrived for their first day of work. I led them into the conference room.

"All right. I'm the editor here. I'm a hardcore newsman. I don't like fluff. You guys need to go out and start cultivating sources. Everyone knows what that means, right? You need to befriend the cashier at the grocery store, the cops, the guy at the newsstand. Those are the people who are going to tip you off to news. But you'll also have to do a lot of digging on your own. Basically, it all comes down to this: you're on a treasure hunt. When you find some, come back here and tell me about it. Then go out and look for some more. Got it?"

They all looked at me in horror. You could smell the fear.

The *Our Times* reporters I managed routinely uncovered interesting news stories in Fullerton and Brea that had statewide and county interest. But none of them could write. I reworked all the reporters' stories and explained to them as patiently as I could the mechanics of the edit.

"See this quote?" I would say. "If you move it up, it makes the story much stronger and backs up what you said in your lede."

Everything I taught them was based on a gut instinct. I wasn't formally educated in the art of writing or editing. I surprised myself by sounding like I knew what I was talking about.

I started to skip the daily A.A. meetings. I didn't have the desire to drink or use drugs, and no longer saw the point in waking up an hour earlier every morning to remind myself of a past I was trying to forget.

As an *Our Times* editor I had to call Jill every morning to discuss the stories I planned to run that day.

"Oooh, that sounds good," Jill would say after I told her about one particular piece. "We'll take that one for the main section."

Times editors, like Jill, viewed *Our Times* as their own personal tip service. *Our Times* reporters would go out and spend hours hunting down news, and if it was a really good story Jill would give it bigger play in the countywide edition. Because the *Our Times* reporters were so inexperienced, Jill would hand off the stories to a *Times* senior reporter. On rare occasions, *Our Times* reporters would be able to work on the story for the real *Times*, but senior reporters hated sharing a byline, so they would usually have the neophyte reporters hand over notes and sources. Then the senior reporters would write up the story without crediting its source. And every time a story was plucked from *Our Times* we were forced to scramble for a replacement piece.

It was a losing battle, but I always fought to get my reporters a byline.

Lennie Laguire, editor of the *Times Orange County* edition, wouldn't allow *Our Times* reporters to write any story that could run in the county edition. This was an order sent around the *Times Orange County* newsroom.

It was my job to explain to a reporter that she can't write her story because the *Times* thinks it's too good to run in *Our Times* and it will run instead on page B1 of the countywide edition. But she can't contribute to the story, either, because the *Times* editors don't think she's good enough to share a byline with a senior reporter.

"Sorry. The *Times* fucked us and they're taking your story. I'm sorry. I feel terrible. I fought for you but they won't budge."

"Umm, I don't understand," said the reporter. "You tell us to go out and find hard news. But when we do, the *Times* takes it from us. So what's the incentive for us to go out and look for stories like this when we won't even get to report them?"

There was no incentive. I knew that. For these first-time reporters, journalism was already leaving a bad taste in their mouths.

We were rolling out new sections of *Our Times* faster than General Motors could produce cars. That's when the shit hit the fan. *Los Angeles Times'* management was criticized for cutting a secret deal with the Staples Center to share advertising revenue the *Times* would get from a magazine devoted to the new arena. *Times* reporters, apparently unaware of the agreement, wrote glowing stories about the stadium. When news of the special arrangement between the *Times* and the Staples Center leaked, there was a revolt within the newspaper. Reporters called for the resignation of CEO Mark Willes and his lieutenant, Kathryn Downing.

Times reporters also denounced Willes' and Downing's plans to increase the *Times'* circulation by one million copies. The

Times' editorial staffers singled out *Our Times*, and demanded that *Our Times* be shut down because it tarnished their integrity by employing inexperienced reporters and running soft news stories. Dozens of newspapers that covered the Staples Center scandal were also critical of *Our Times*.

I became so incensed by the criticism of *Our Times* that I called *The New York Times'* Felicity Barringer to complain. Barringer wrote a story about Willes and Downing that said *Our Times* reporters "do little more than rewrite press releases."

"Felicity, this is Jason Leopold, city editor for *Our Times*. I don't know where you're getting your information but *Our Times* reporters don't rewrite press releases. They're out on the front lines digging for news, and when they find something good they're forced to hand over their notes to the senior reporters at the *Times*. That's what's going on behind the scenes, Felicity. Do you think that's ethical? Do you?" I asked on her voicemail.

I blew the whistle because we all feared that *Our Times* would be shut down and we would lose our jobs. A couple of minutes later my phone rang.

"Hi, Jason, this is Felicity Barringer with *The New York Times*," she said, in a voice so deep that I thought for a second that Felicity must be trans.

"Oh, jeez, hi," I said. "I actually didn't think you would call back."

"I appreciate your message and will look into what you said about *Our Times*."

She never did follow up the story. And that wasn't my last run-in with Felicity Barringer.

Bill Lobdell said I was doing such a good editing job that he wanted me to start editing a weekly religion column for the main edition of the *Times*. Bill and I started to get together outside of the office and discovered that we shared a common interest in Howard Stern. My impression of Stern's producer Gary Dell'abate, also known as "Baba Booey," reduced Bill to tears.

"Hey boff, it's me, your editor, fla fla flo flee," I would say to Bill when I called him on my way to the office, in my best Baba Booey voice. "Today's we's goings to write a story 'bout my big teeth and my pus-filled gums…"

My Baba Booey routine would be put on speakerphone for the other *Pilot* office editors. It was those little things—jokes, lunches, and going to a restaurant after work with the editorial staff—that made it fun to go to work every day. But the *Times* continued to poach our best stories and *Our Times* always seemed to have serious copyediting and design errors. Often a caption would appear underneath the wrong picture.

Bill hired a woman from the *Register* named Deniene to edit the newest edition of *Our Times* for Anaheim, home to Disneyland, a baseball stadium, and not much else. Deniene's desk was situated next to mine. She was a control freak who wouldn't let anyone assist her with editing and demanded to have a say in the design of her page. Deniene spoke to her reporters like they were her children.

"Now, David, what did I tell you about filing your story after deadline?" she would say to a twenty-year-old reporter who always finished his stories late. "Is that fair to the others?"

"I didn't mean it, Deniene," David would say, hanging his head in shame. "I won't do it again."

I tended to treat my reporters like my father treated me.

"Veronica, did your mother smoke crack before she gave birth to you?" I would say to a reporter after she filed too many unintelligible stories that were sometimes written partially in Spanish.

Deniene and I were good cop and bad cop. She nurtured her reporters. I verbally abused mine. She stroked their hair. I threw things at them. It wasn't all an act, though. Ever since I stopped going to A.A. meetings I was on edge. The 300 milligrams of antidepressants I took every morning weren't doing the trick. I couldn't stand being inside of my own skin. I felt like I had a whole lot of rage bottled up inside of me, and all I needed was a reason to let it burst.

Also fueling my anger were Deniene's kids; she brought them to the office at least three times a week. I warned her that a newsroom was not a good place to bring a three-year-old boy and four-year-old girl.

"Why not?" she asked.

"There's a lot of cursing," I said.

Deniene turned the office into a mini day-care center, complete with a duffel bag full of dolls, toy trucks, blocks, crayons, pillows, blankets, and books.

As the 5:00 p.m. deadline rolled around, I gave Deniene's kids a lesson in vulgarity out of spite.

"Motherfucking son of a bitch hurry up and file your stories you fucking hacks!" I shouted to reporters while slamming a hammer on my desk. I kept the hammer on top of my computer and used it to get reporters' attention whenever they missed deadline.

This must have startled the children because they started to cry. Deniene tried to quiet them but it was no use. Their crying became louder and started to disturb some reporters who were still trying to quickly complete their stories.

"Hey, Deniene, can you do something about that?" a reporter shouted. Deniene glared at me, gave me the finger, then took her kids into Bill's office and shut the door. About ten minutes later she walked out with the toys and the duffel bag. Bill said he gave her permission to work from home where she could keep a better eye on her children.

For the next several months, Deniene spent two days a week working from home. And I was becoming impatient with the way things were turning out. I couldn't get Bill to put his foot down and demand that the *Times* stop poaching our best news stories. I was working twelve-hour days. The future of *Our Times* was uncertain.

I started to search the Internet for other reporting jobs and found a listing for Dow Jones Newswires. The company was looking for a bureau chief to report on energy issues. The office was located two miles from my apartment in Los Angeles. I didn't know anything about energy, but I applied anyway.

I brought in some jazz records to help calm my rage.

Charles Mingus' "Pork Pie Hat" was spinning when I got an email demand from Deniene asking me to turn off the music. How the fuck did she know I was playing music? She was working at home, after all.

"One of my reporters sent an e-mail saying he can't concentrate because your music is too loud," she wrote.

"Your reporter doesn't have the balls to ask me personally to lower the volume?" I asked her in an e-mail response.

"He's afraid of you," she wrote back.

I felt the blood inside my body start to boil and like Mount St. Helens, I erupted.

"WHO THE FUCK TOLD DENIENE THAT MY MUSIC IS TOO LOUD? WHICH ONE OF YOU ASSHOLES DOESN'T HAVE THE BALLS TO SAY IT TO MY FACE?" I shouted across the entire newsroom.

"It was me!" said David, a scrawny five-foot-two reporter. "What are you gonna do about it?"

"I'll rip your fucking head off your shoulders, you little prick," I fired back, spittle coming out of my mouth.

Just then, one of the copy editors jumped in between us and held me back. "Take a deep breath," he said.

I walked outside and chain-smoked three cigarettes. Perhaps I shouldn't have stopped going to A.A. meetings. I went back into the office, finished my editing, and took off to a journalism convention in Las Vegas.

The Society of Professional Journalists sponsored the Vegas convention. I attended our local chapter's monthly meetings and was passionate about getting to know other working journalists and doing what I could to assist the organization.

The Los Angeles chapter voted me to become their president, saying that I "lived and breathed" journalism. It didn't seem right, though, to have a felon head a professional journalism organization. I momentarily distracted myself from fear of my past and called Bill to tell him the news.

"Hey boff, I is da new president of da Sooo-ciety of Prufessional Journalists," I said as Baba Booey. "Whatcha tink of dat, boff?"

"I got bad news," Bill replied. "You're suspended for a week without pay because of the incident with David. He and Deniene reported you to Human Resources."

"What the fuck! Are you serious? Why?"

"They both said you became threatening when Deniene asked you to turn down your music," Bill said.

"That's fucked up, Bill. David should be suspended, too."

"He's not," Bill said. "I asked David and Deniene to let me handle it but they said they were going to Human Resources because you and I are friends."

"HR is going to interview your staff to decide if they want you to come back to work here. Deniene also told them that you and I hang out after work, and they're also looking at whether I didn't discipline you when you have your outbursts in the newsroom. I'm going to be editing your paper during your suspension."

I fucked up my life again. I didn't deserve to live. My heart was pounding. I felt like someone snuck up behind me and hit me over the head with a baseball bat. Las Vegas was the wrong town for me to be in right then. Alcohol was everywhere and I could easily score coke. But deep down I knew that if I started again with all that I would die in Vegas. I couldn't do that to Lisa. I called my A.A. sponsor and asked him for some advice.

"Go to a meeting," he said. "And don't drink and use no matter what."

Turns out there are A.A. meetings around the clock in Vegas. But I didn't bother going to one.

I went to my hotel room and stared at the ceiling. I was worried that I would relapse if I stayed in Vegas any longer, so I told the members of my local SPJ chapter that I accepted the presidency but I had to leave because of a family emergency. They hugged me and told me to be safe.

Was God testing me to see if I could handle bad news without turning to drugs to numb the pain and the guilt?

"I passed, God," I said aloud on my drive home. "I passed with flying colors. Can you please make sure I don't lose my job? I won't let this happen again"

I often spoke to God when things got bad. Sometimes he listened. Sometimes not.

It took me four hours to get home. I was in a daze the whole way. Lisa was still awake when I got to our apartment at about 1:00 a.m.

"What are you doing here?" she asked, dropping a magazine to the floor with a loud plop.

"I got suspended from work for threatening a reporter." I was so ashamed I didn't look into her eyes.

"Oh, Jason," she said, disappointed. "What happened?"

"I just lost my temper," I said, refusing to go into details.

"Are you going to lose your job?"

"No way. They won't survive without me."

"You need to go into therapy," Lisa said. "You have way too many issues you need to deal with. I want you to find a therapist immediately."

Bill called me the next morning and said I should go to the main office at the *Times*.

I put on a suit and drove to Costa Mesa and met with two of the *Times'* human resources representatives. I was surprised to see Bill there.

"Jason, I don't know how to tell you this, but I've got to let you go," he said. "I'm sorry."

One of the human resources representatives told me that the company has a zero tolerance policy against violence and threats against other employees.

I put on sunglasses to hide the tears that started to pour out of my eyes. "I mean, I never planned on walking over to that reporter and twisting his head until it came off of his shoulders. I just lost my temper. I'm sorry. Please give me another chance."

"It's out of our control, Mr. Leopold," the human resources rep said. "You should, however, watch your temper."

The HR rep said she would have likely let me off with a warning, but she spent two days interviewing reporters, and they all said they were afraid of me. They said I was a bully.

"From what I understand, you keep a hammer on top of your computer, and you swing it to intimidate the staff. I also understand that you frequently use obscenities when you speak to employees. There's no room for that type of behavior at the *Times*," she said.

This was the second news job I was fired from in twenty-four months. What's the point in being sober? I'll never work again. I always make the same mistakes. I'll never learn. I couldn't stop crying.

Bill stood up, shook my hand, and gave me a hug.

"Take care of yourself," he said. "We'll miss you."

That was it. No severance, no goodbye party, nothing to commemorate my nearly two years at the *Times*.

I wasn't sure if I would make it home alive. I started to have suicidal thoughts. That always happened when my world started closing in on me. I first tried to commit suicide at the age of five; I tried slicing open my veins on the wrong side of my wrist, and my father told me I was stupid, showing me the correct way to hold the knife and proper way to do the deed.

Now I would have to deal with pain and guilt without the help of drugs and alcohol. I wanted to anesthetize myself so badly.

When I stumbled to my car, tears pouring down my face, I found a message on my cell phone.

"Hi, Jason. This is Arden Dale, managing editor at Dow Jones Newswires in New York. We got your resume and clips. Very impressive. I am eager to talk to you about the bureau chief position. Please call me when you have a free moment."

EIGHT

I GUESS THE MAXIM IS true: whenever one door closes another one opens.

I scribbled down Arden's phone number in my notebook and drove out of the *Times* parking lot for the last time. I used my shirtsleeve to wipe away my tears, took a deep breath, and called her.

"Arden Dale."

"Arden, hi, this is Jason Leopold. I'm returning your call." My voice was still shaky. I bit my lip to keep from crying. I was just starting to absorb the shock from getting fired from the *Times*, worrying that I would never write again.

"Hi, Jason. Thanks for calling back so quickly. I'm very impressed by your clips and your experience. You've really climbed the ladder the past four years. So you're currently the city editor for the *Los Angeles Times*?"

My resume said I worked for the *Los Angeles Times* and that I was city editor, which, in a sense, was true. In small print I wrote that I was responsible for the *Times'* community news coverage, that I managed twelve reporters, and so on. I hoped Arden wouldn't bother to read the details. When it came to my education, the resume further lied, saying that I had a bachelor's degree in journalism. Luckily, no one asked to see verification.

"Yes," I said to Arden. "I was promoted to city editor after two months and was hand-picked to help the *Times* launch its community news division in Orange County."

"Well, I'm curious," Arden said. "Why do you want to leave? It sounds like you're doing very well at the *Times*."

I had to think fast. I considered my ability to lie at any given moment a gift. Lying was about survival. When I was a teenager, my dad would come home and ask me if I walked the dog. I was afraid if I told him the truth he would hit me. So I said, "Yeah, Dad, I walked him." But then I would take the lie a step further by describing my dog's shit as being like diarrhea, and warned my dad about feeding the dog correctly. The scheme worked.

"Well, Arden, I miss the fast-paced world of newswires," I said. "As you can see on my resume, I worked for a newswire a couple of years ago and it was a great experience. My personality lends itself to that kind of environment. I'm a hustler. I love to break news. I get off on it."

"I know what you mean," she said. "That's why I like working here. Well, I'll tell you what, I'm going to call your former employers. Is it possible to speak with someone at the *Times*?"

"Uh, uh, I don't think so," I said, worried she'd find out about me being terminated. "They don't know I've applied for another job and would probably be upset if they found out. But let me see if I can get an editor to speak with you off the record."

"Yes, please. I would need to speak to someone at the *Times* about you," she said.

I had a good feeling that I would get this job if I could get Bill to give me a reference. I called him on his cell phone.

"Hey, Bill, it's Jason." I hoped that emotional timbre of my voice would make him feel guilty enough to call Arden and say nice things about me.

"How are you holding up?" he asked.

"I'm still in shock," I said. "But listen, I have a favor to ask."

"Shoot."

"I have an opportunity to get another job immediately, and I need you to call this woman and give me a reference."

"Jason, you just got fired. I got a lot of heat from HR. I can't lie and tell this person that you weren't fired. If it gets back to HR I'm screwed. I've got a family to think about."

"But you know I did a good job," I said. "Just go into your office, close your door, and do what's right," I said. "No one will ever be the wiser."

"I just can't take that chance," he said.

"You know what you are, Bill? You're not a man. You're a fucking pussy. You traded in your balls for a fucking job. I won't forget this, you fucking slave," I shouted into the phone.

I punched the steering wheel and my rearview mirror, which busted off its hinge, and screamed "FUUUUUCK" at the top of my lungs. I could feel the blood inside my veins start to boil.

I asked Jill if she could speak to Arden.

"Absolutely," she said. "I'm so sorry to hear about what happened. I believe you were screwed really bad by this company."

"Thanks, Jill. Oh, this woman doesn't know I was fired, so please don't say anything," I said.

"I won't."

I left a message on Arden's voicemail telling her to call Jill Jones for a reference. I pulled into my garage and ran into my house. Lisa was at work. I didn't bother calling her to tell her that I was fired; I hoped that I would get the job at Dow Jones by the end of the day. Then I could tell her the bad news and good news all at once and not have to deal with the disappointment she would feel over my getting fired.

My answering machine was blinking. I pressed the playback button to listen to the messages. There were twelve.

"Jason, hey, it's Leslie. I am so sorry to hear about everything that happened. I hope you're doing well. You will be so missed here. If there is anything I can do, please call me."

"Jason, it's Jasmine. I just heard the news. I am so upset by all of this. I want you to know that you are a great editor and a great reporter and I learned so much from you. I also want you to know that I went into Bill's office a little while ago and bawled him out. This is so unfair. I'll miss you."

"Jason, it's Greg. Man, you got fucked. The newsroom won't be the same without you. Let me know if I can help you, my man."

"Jason, it's Nancy. Everyone here loves you. I want you to know that. You are such a great person and you brought life to this office. I wrote a letter to Human Resources about you. I e-mailed you a copy. Everyone here is in shock."

The rest of the messages on my answering machine were equally supportive. I had no idea I left such a lasting impression on the other reporters I worked with. What was it about me that they liked? I thought about it for quite some time but couldn't figure it out.

I checked my e-mail and downloaded the letter Nancy, the page designer who worked at the *Daily Pilot*, wrote to Human Resources on my behalf.

Cyndy Chrispell
Human Resources
Times Orange County
1375 Sunflower Ave.
Costa Mesa, ca 92626

April 4, 2000

Dear Cyndy,

I feel impelled to write to you after the sudden departure of my colleague, Jason Leopold, from our company. It is my understanding that Jason was fired Monday after being suspended for allegedly threatening a co-worker.

I have not been asked to write to you. In fact, l am not writing this in an attempt to reinstate Jason or even to tell you what he did was not wrong. I am writing to you because our company, *Times Community News*, has suffered a tremendous loss.

To our benefit, Jason was overqualified for his position as city editor of the Fullerton/area *Our Times*, a section of the *Orange County Times*. He is a consummate journalist in every sense of the word, a respected writer, and an impeccable editor with keen news judgment— in general, a great guy with an amazing sense of humor.

Jason is the president of the Society for Professional Journalists, Los Angeles Chapter, and in that capacity has been interviewed on radio and television programs as well as various newspapers. He has written for numerous national publications. In short, he was a wonderful ambassador for our company.

He also headed our company's ethics committee; of which I am a member, and often said—as many of us do—that he felt working at *TCN* was like being part of a big family.

I was not involved in and do not know the details of what happened to Jason over the past week. I just know that whatever he may have done, it could not have been as bad as the loss that we must now endure.

As you can surely imagine, I am extremely troubled and saddened by Jason's departure. Our company will not be whole without him.

Sincerely,
Nancy Cheever
Features Editor
Daily Pilot/Times Community News

Nancy's letter made me teary. I felt like I didn't deserve her kind words because I was such a liar about my past. Would Nancy and everyone else still feel the same way about me if they knew the truth? I doubted it.

My phone kept on ringing. I didn't answer it. Then Bill called.

I stood in front of the answering machine silent, as if Bill could hear me breathing.

"Guess you're not around. I wanted to let you know that you could have that woman call Tony Dodero at the *Pilot*. I spoke to him and he will give a reference for you. All right? Take care. Bye."

Tony Dodero was the editor of the *Daily Pilot*, a hardcore newsman like me. He loved the rush of breaking news, hated whiny reporters, and could totally rewrite a story in less than ten minutes. We would often talk about our reporting experiences whenever he caught me smoking a cigarette in the *Pilot* parking lot. He was the kind of guy you'd want to go into combat with.

I called Arden to give her Tony's number.

"Hi Arden, it's Jason Leopold. I'm sorry to bother you but I have another person at the *Times* you can speak to about me."

"Great. I spoke to Kathleen, the city editor you worked for at the *Whittier Daily News,* and she said some nice things about you. But when I called the editor you worked for at City News Service she wouldn't say anything about you. She would only confirm that you worked for the company. Did something happen there?" Arden asked suspiciously.

"Hmm, very strange. Well, I believe City News has a policy of only confirming employment. I don't think they're allowed to go into details because they worry they'll get sued," I said.

"Yes, I do know that's a concern for some employers," she said. That was a lie. City News had no such policy.

When I didn't hear from Arden for two days after that, I interpreted the delay as a sign that maybe Arden was doing a background check. I became manic. I must have left her a dozen messages in forty-eight hours.

"Hi, Arden, it's Jason Leopold calling. Hope all is well. Just checking in..."

"Hey, Arden, Jason Leopold here. Just going through my clips. I found another batch that you may be interested in. Let me know if you want me to fax them to you."

"Arden, hey there, it's Jason Leopold. I've been doing a little research on deregulation. That's the beat you said I would be responsible for, right? Anyway, I have some good ideas for feature stories. Give me a call and I'll discuss it with you."

"Hi, Arden, it's Jason Leopold again. Listen, I hope I'm not being a pest, but I just wanted to see if you made a decision yet. Okay, hopefully I'll speak to you soon."

"Hi, Arden, it's Jason Leopold. Just wanna make sure you got the messages I left for you yesterday. Speak to you soon."

Maybe I shouldn't have called so many times, I thought to myself as I paced around my living room, imagining her horrified reaction as she played back all twelve messages.

I called a few friends to get their opinions. They all confirmed to me that I sounded like a desperate sociopath. I once again called Arden back and when it kicked into her voicemail I pressed the pound button on my phone.

"Meridian mail," the recorded female voice said. "Please enter your password."

Hoping to bust into Arden's voicemail and erase some of the messages I left her, I came up with a simple numerical combination I thought Arden may have chosen as her password.

"Your password is not valid. Please try again."

I tried more numerical combinations, but still no luck.

My obsession with trying to get in touch with Arden was also inspired by my wife Lisa's insistence that I start seeing a therapist. She said I kept repeating the same old patterns in my life—getting fired, legal problems, fits of rage—and instead of dealing with my problems I ran away from them. She said that no matter how great I believed the next reporting job I get would be, I'll still have the same old issues, and I'll repeat the same mistakes unless I get professional help.

"Uh-uh," I said. "Not true. It'll be different this time."

The truth is I avoided therapy. I was afraid that I'd learn the truth about myself, and it would be ugly. Maybe I would be forced to talk about my mother and father, and how if they were ever killed in a car accident, a plane crash, or some other type of disaster I wouldn't cry. What if I had to talk about my guilt about turning into a drug addict? Or my shame about being a bed wetter, my felony conviction, and the entire assortment of depressing thoughts that I had successfully disconnected myself from? I didn't want anyone to know how I really felt. I certainly didn't want to feel those things anymore. I already swallowed a handful of antidepressants on a daily basis to help me get out of bed in the morning. I knew that if I could just score this job at Dow Jones everything would be perfect.

"You'll see, Lisa," I said. "Trust me."

Three days later, I finally got a call from Arden.

"Jason?" she asked. "It's Arden Dale. I guess it's true what I've heard about you."

"Oh yeah? What's that?"

"That you are a very aggressive reporter. I have to admit, after listening to all of the messages you left me, I'd have to agree," Arden said.

"Listen, about that, I'm sorry I…"

"Don't be sorry. We've been looking for someone who can reshape the L.A. bureau and take charge. I figure you're either a really great journalist or a serial killer. So we'd like to offer you the job as L.A. bureau chief of Dow Jones Newswires. You'll be in charge of our L.A. office and you'll be managing two reporters."

"Oh Arden. You made my day. This is the perfect job. The office is about two miles from my house. This is just so perfect. Oh my God, my wife is going to be thrilled. I assume you'll want to meet me. Does that mean you're going to fly me to New York?"

"No. We'll do this over the phone. We'll meet sometime down the road when you come to New York. I need to know what your salary was at the *Los Angeles Times*."

When I left the *Times*, I was making 42,000 dollars a year. I lied to Arden.

"Fifty-five thousand" I said.

"Well, the bureau chief position pays sixty K. So you'll be getting a five thousand-dollar raise plus benefits," she said.

This was the most money I've ever earned…legitimately. "That's great. I accept."

"Excellent. I feel really good about this. I'm going to send you out an offer letter and have someone from Human Resources contact you. Can you start next week?"

"I can start tomorrow if you want."

"Next week is fine. Congratulations, Jason. I'm looking forward to working with you."

Unbelievable. I was just hired by one of the largest news organizations in the world, the same company that publishes *The Wall Street Journal*, whose reporters specialize in knowing every detail about the people and industries they cover. The irony of this is that no one at Dow Jones knew anything about me. This was too weird. I actually could have been a serial killer and I still would have been hired at the *Los Angeles Times* and Dow Jones Newswires because no one bothered to do a background check. Makes you wonder whether journalism has its Jeffrey Dahmers.

A couple of days later I got a package from Dow Jones. Inside was a letter from Arden formally offering me the bureau chief job.

Dear Jason:

Congratulations and welcome to Dow Jones Newswires. This letter is to confirm your hire as Los Angeles Bureau Chief at a base salary of $60,000.

Sincerely,
Arden Dale
Managing Editor

Also inside the package was an employee application that I had to fill out, despite the fact that most of the questions on it, such as my past employers, were already answered on the resume I sent to Arden. In longhand, I filled out my work history on the form. I also had to provide reasons I left the companies I once worked for. What was I supposed to say? That I was fired because I threatened to kill a reporter during my stint at the *Los Angeles Times*? That I was let go because of a libel suit when I worked for City News? To cover things up I invented a few stories.

"Decided to pursue a freelance writing career while I worked on the Great American Novel," I wrote about leaving City News.

"I missed the fast-paced world of breaking news," was what I said about leaving the *Times*.

On the last page of the application was that annoying question that had dogged me for years.

"Have you ever been convicted of a felony?"

This time, however, the question came with a caveat.

"Answering 'yes' does not automatically disqualify you from the interview process or from being considered for employment at Dow Jones & Co."

Bullshit. I would never be hired as a reporter if I copped to my past crimes. There were probably hundreds of other reporters who applied for this job, and I'll bet none of them have a rap sheet. What incentive does a news organization have to hire a convicted felon? Would there be a full disclosure statement at the end of every story I wrote that says, "Jason Leopold, convicted of grand larceny?" All I wanted was a chance to report the truth, but in order to do that I had to lie, again.

I considered coming clean, and for a moment, I actually did. My conscience guided the black ballpoint pen toward the first tiny square marked "yes." I neatly colored in the box, keeping the ink within the lines of the small square so as not to draw too much attention to my answer. I put the pen down and stared at the application for a few seconds. Then a little devil appeared on my right shoulder, jabbing my ear with his pitchfork.

You're crazy. You'll never get this job if you tell them about the felony. Think about it. You're a criminal. How many criminals do you know working in journalism?

The pitchfork-bearing bastard had a point. What the hell was I doing, checking off the "yes" box? I immediately colored in the "no" box on the application, this time using a black felt tip pen. The ink was much darker than the ink from the ballpoint pen in the "yes" box.

But I couldn't just send back the application to the Dow Jones human resources department by answering yes and no to the felony question. So my pen skated around the back page of the application, making figure eights all around the page until the answer to the felony question, as well as several others, was blurred by thick lines of black ink. At first glance, the last page of the application looked like a child doodled on it. On the top right corner of the application I wrote a short prayer in Hebrew in tiny letters that my grandfather, a holocaust survivor, taught me when I was about five years old.

"Baruch Hashem," which, translated into English, means "with the help of God."

I put the application in the return envelope along with the benefits paperwork I filled out, crossed my fingers, and mailed it back to Arden at the Dow Jones Jersey City office. I don't think Arden, her boss, or anyone in Dow Jones' personnel department ever bothered to look at my application.

NINE

NEWS SERVICES TRY GET an accurate story out on the wire before the others. That's how you get people to subscribe. Why settle for *Bloomberg* or Reuters when you can get your news faster from Dow Jones? Sure, sometimes *Bloomberg* and Reuters only trail Dow Jones by a minute or two and vice versa, but that minute translates into multimillion-dollar gains or losses for Wall Street investors, who depend on getting news as soon as possible to make investment decisions.

The only thing I knew about electricity when I started working at Dow Jones Newswires in April 2000 was that AC/DC didn't mean Antichrist/Devil's Child. But the great thing about working in journalism, particularly for a wire service where every second counts, is that you're forced to figure it all out while you're writing a story. You have no choice but to report the news as you get it. You could write about the toughest subjects even if, as my father used to say, you don't know shit from shinola.

You should know, of course, the nuts and bolts of journalism 101: lede, nut graf, and so on. But the more stories you write on your beat, the faster you pick up the subject. The hands-on experience is more valuable than a college degree.

I was surprised how much I enjoyed writing about the electricity racket, and how eager I was to learn about the subject. I'm the kind of person who craves knowledge. If you lock me in a room with a bunch of doctors for a month I might eventually be able to fake brain surgery. A month after I was hired at Dow Jones, I was already getting positive feedback on my stories. I spent a lot of my free time reading about AB1890, the law California's legislature passed in 1996 that deregulated the state's electricity industry, forcing the commodity to be bought and sold in the free market. California was the first state to deregulate its electricity market. Many other states took a wait-and-see approach before following California's lead, to see if deregulation would, in fact, give consumers a break on their utility bills, which is what the energy industry promised when it pitched the idea to politicians.

My early stories were mostly insider pieces, such as company X is building a power plant or transmission lines need to be repaired. Within three months, I churned out so many scoops on California's experiment with deregulation that Dow Jones Newswires used my name and one of my exclusive reports in a *The Wall Street Journal* advertisement. It was surreal. My coworkers showered me with compliments and my editor rewarded me with cash bonuses.

I got my first big scoop three weeks after I started working at Dow Jones. Fishing for a story, I had spent the better part of a month introducing myself to CEOs, company spokespeople, state agency reps, and Wall Street analysts who covered the energy industry.

One person I called regularly was Jesus Arredondo, the spokesman for the California Power Exchange, or CALPX for short. All the electricity trading in the state had to go through the CALPX. That was the law.

Jesus knew everyone. He spent a few years working as the press secretary to Gray Davis' predecessor, Pete Wilson, a Republican, who signed AB1890 into law. He gave me a crash course in state politics and answered all of my questions about deregulation and explained the difference between a kilowatt and a megawatt. He gave me the names and numbers of lawmakers in California, mostly Republicans, whom I could use as sources and hooked me up with the movers and shakers in the energy industry. About a week after I started, Jesus told me he'd soon have a big story for me to report, one that would catch everyone's attention.

"Just be patient, man," he said to me on the phone as I, in a manic state, pressed him for details. "I'm giving you this story. It'll be an exclusive. Don't worry."

I couldn't comprehend what big news would come out of the power industry and I couldn't stop obsessing about the story. I called Jesus everyday.

Later that month, I went to Dow Jones' New Jersey headquarters to meet Arden and the rest of the staff that covered the energy industry for Newswires. The company put me up in a hotel a block away from the World Trade Center. It was the first time I had gone back to New York since I got sober and pleaded guilty to a felony. It was two years since the rats-in-my-pants and the City News debacle. I hadn't had a drink or a line of coke since. I was nervous being in New York; just knowing that I could go to one of my old hangout spots and score some coke made my body twitch and my teeth chatter. I felt like I was going through withdrawal all over again. But I didn't dare go near my old stomping grounds. I was particularly paranoid about running into Lenny and Bruno and Maury. I also was afraid of bumping into former coworkers from Milan.

Two blocks away from the hotel I was staying in was The Tombs, where I spent a week after I got arrested. Now I was in a swank Manhattan hotel room wearing a suit and tie and hanging out with people who work on Wall Street. I'd gone legit. I'd turned my life around. Yet still I felt like I was living in the Witness Protection Program, still running away from my past and scared that I would be exposed. Everyone I commiserated with in my new life told me that I seemed like a nice Jewish boy from upstate New York. Man, if they only knew.

Voices are deceiving. When you talk on the telephone to someone you've never met, you often visualize how they look in person. Most of the time, you create a picture in your head that has no basis in reality. I pictured Arden Dale to be a tall, leggy blonde who wore bright red lipstick on perky lips. I'm not sure how that image got into my head; such appearances are rare in the world of print journalism. In reality, Arden was in her forties, five-foot five with curly salt-and-pepper hair. She dressed like a tomboy and walked like a guy. She lived in suburban New Jersey with her husband and two-year-old son. She helped Dow Jones launch its energy service. As a reporter she wrote about the subject in the mid-'90s, working her way up to managing editor. Both of us were fiercely competitive.

My other boss at Dow Jones was Andrew Dowell, a tall guy in his thirties who seemed to have some kind of attention deficit disorder. Andrew drifted away in the midst of a conversation and would talk about other things before he would make his point. If you called him about one of your stories, he'd sometimes leave you on hold for ten minutes, and then he'd restart the conversation, saying, "Sorry, dude." If there were an award for slowest editor, Andrew would win hands down.

Mark Golden also covered electricity for Dow Jones, and had a talent for turning technical information on the electricity industry into plain English. He wrote a weekly column called "Power Points," which he used, at times, as a platform to talk about the benefits of deregulation. The four of us, Arden, Andrew, Mark, and I, were the reporting squad responsible for covering electricity in the United States for the financial community.

The Dow Jones Jersey City office was located right on the edge of the Hudson River. It had an awesome view of the New York City skyline. Each morning while I was there, I'd leave the PATH train and walk outside the subway station, staring at the World Trade Center and the Empire State Building across the river before I started work. It was like admiring a painting. I had never realized how beautiful the Manhattan skyline was, never took advantage of it all those years I lived there.

When the terrorists flew the jets into the World Trade Center on 9/11, Mark told me that the Dow Jones office building shook and everyone in the office thought it was an earthquake. He said the Dow Jones employees put their faces and hands against the sixth floor windows and watched in horror as the buildings crumbled.

When I checked my voicemail, Jesus left a message.

"Hey, Jason, it's Jesus. I'm ready to give you the exclusive as promised," he said, "We literally just finished working on the details. Call me when you get this message."

My body started to tremble, like it did back in the days when I knew I was close to scoring coke. It was the score that I got off on most.

I took out a fresh notebook from my knapsack, flipped it open, and wrote "Exclusive from Jesus" on the first page. I underlined those words a few times. Then I picked up the phone and called him.

"Jesus Arredondo"

"Got chur message, bro. Break it down for me."

"Okay. You ready?"

"Yup."

"In February of 1999, a market participant alerted the PX's market monitoring committee to some strange activity that took place regarding one of the transmission lines. We've determined that an out-of-state seller violated the rules for trading electricity by submitting a bid into the market for 2900 megawatts to be carried on a transmission line that has a rated capacity of fifteen megawatts."

"Jesus, I have no fucking idea what you're talking about," I said, somewhat frustrated by all of the technical details. "Can you explain this in English?"

"Basically, what it comes down to is this company tried to fit an elephant through a keyhole. They were manipulating the market so they could make more money."

"What company was this?"

"Enron."

That was the first time I ever heard of Enron.

I soon discovered that Enron was the Studio 54 of corporate America—the epitome of mega-corp decadence. I heard rumors of strippers roaming the halls and all-night parties at hotels and bars. Enron was all about excess. It was more, more, more, now, now, now. Naturally, I was intrigued by those stories of gluttony. Although socially I remained a liberal, working at Dow Jones quickly transformed me into a pro-business, free-market conservative. I thought of Enron and the people who worked there as celebrities.

Enron was based in Houston, Texas, and is credited for influencing California and several other states to deregulate its electricity markets. It did so by promising consumers that they would save tens of billions of dollars if they could choose to buy their electricity from a variety of energy companies, as opposed to being stuck with their crusty old utility, which Enron claimed charged customers an arm and a leg for power because it was the only game in town. The idea was sold as similar to the breakup of Ma Bell. Enron was hoping to scoop up most of California's retail electricity consumers once the doors to competition opened, by promising better service and cheaper rates than the local utility could provide.

Enron spent twenty-five million dollars on a marketing campaign promoting deregulation, and produced a commercial that aired during the 1998 Super Bowl. Retail choice, the cornerstone of electrical deregulation, was a miserable failure. Consumers never bothered to look for an alternative electricity provider. The way they saw it, "If it ain't broke, don't fix it."

I wasn't convinced that the information I was getting from Jesus would make a good story. It seemed too technical. And I didn't really understand what Enron had done wrong and what impact the company's actions had on the financial community, the Dow Jones Newswires audience.

"Deliberately congesting the transmission line could have caused power prices to go up, and it could also cause a blackout," Jesus explained to me, "because we can't send power from point A to point B. You see, Enron owns the rights to that transmission line so we sort of rent it from them to send power back and forth, and if there's traffic on the line we have to pay Enron a lot of money to clear the traffic to keep the power flowing. Ultimately, that money is charged back to the utility and the utility bills the consumer. What it comes down to is Enron looked for a way to make money. They purposely tried to clog the transmission line knowing that we'd have to pay them to free up the line so we could keep the power flowing and avoid blackouts. It's a clear case of manipulating the system for financial gain."

My head started to hurt. I couldn't comprehend the meaning of all of this. I planned on asking Mark Golden to translate what Jesus said to me after I got off the phone.

"So what are you guys doing about this manipulation or whatever you call it?" I asked Jesus.

"Well, first of all, you need to understand that this is the first case of manipulation we found since California officially deregulated in 1998," Jesus said. "We're taking action against Enron 'cause we want to send a message out to the other energy companies that trade power. Just because our market is young and imperfect doesn't mean you can get away with this type of behavior."

"Okay. What action?"

"Enron is going to pay a 25,000-dollar fine to settle this," Jesus said, "and promise that they won't do it again. I'll fax you a copy of the settlement."

"Cool. I'm gonna also call Enron for a comment."

"Can you call me back and let me know what they said?"

"Yeah. No problem."

When I told Mark the nature of my story he freaked.

"Holy shit!" he said, flailing his arms. "That's a major story."

"It is?"

"Shit yeah. You don't understand. Enron's been pushing for deregulation because they say it will lower prices, and then they're fucking California in the ass when no one's looking and trying to jack up prices."

"Okay?"

"Jason, you just got the story of the year," Mark said.

"I did?"

"Dude, your story is going to prove that the market can be fucked with. No one has been able to do that. Believe me, a lot of people have tried. Everyone in the country is watching to see how deregulation works in California before they start to deregulate. California is fucked. They should've designed a better market. They left too many regulations in place. It's not really competitive at all."

"Fuck. I had no idea."

Mark hooked me up with the name and telephone number for Enron's spokesman, Mark Palmer. I called Palmer at his office in Houston and introduced myself.

"Hi, Mark," I said in a high-pitched voice that usually came up when I had to tell someone that I was going to write a negative story about them.

"My name is Jason Leopold. I'm the new bureau chief for Dow Jones Newswires in Los Angeles. But I'm actually calling you from New Jersey. Heh-heh."

"Well, welcome aboard, Jason," Mark said. "What can I do for you?"

"Well, I hate to do this," I said, trying to insinuate I cared about him and Enron so he would feel relaxed and be forthcoming with me. "I know we just met, but this story just fell into my lap so I have no choice..."

"Sure," Mark said. "I understand."

"Well, I just got off the phone with the CALPX, and they said Enron paid a 25,000-dollar fine for breaking some rule that has to do with electricity trading and clogging the transmission line. Can I get a comment from you 'bout that?"

"That's bullshit!" Mark shouted into the phone. "I can't believe the PX is making a federal case about this. We paid the twenty-five grand to cover the PX's costs for investigating this. Enron did not admit any guilt."

"Okay, I understand," I said. "Is what you just told me for the record?"

"Yeah. You can quote me on that."

"Well, what's the deal, Mark? Sounds like there's something going on with Enron and the PX."

"The PX is singling out Enron because we compete with them. Enron also has a trading platform. It's called Enron Online and we want people to use that when they're trading instead of the PX."

"What about the claims that you guys clogged the transmission line?"

"Jason, I can tell you that there were 1,400 separate instances of that in the past year and the PX is only penalizing Enron. That's why I said they're singling us out. Look, this market is crying out for more power and we're doing everything we can to deliver it. We're not manipulating."

Mark Golden helped me translate the technical parts of my notes and I wrote up the story. I didn't bother to call Jesus back because I wanted to get the story out on the wire and be done with it. It didn't feel like I got the juicy story I was hoping for. It felt like I bought some bad coke, snorted it, and didn't get high.

On May 3, 2000, the headline: "Calif. Finds Enron Violated Pwr Transmission Rules" ran across the Dow Jones Newswires. My 615 word story said Enron manipulated the market and purposefully tried to clog the Silver Peak transmission line, which runs from California's Central Valley to San Diego, in order to boost wholesale electricity prices and Enron's bottom line.

I didn't know it then, but it would take nearly two years to the day my story on Enron was first published before it made any kind of an impact. This would be the story that federal energy regulators and investigators, congressmen, and senators would point to after Enron's bankruptcy to prove that the company devised a scheme to rip off California. Turns out that I wrote the first story ever published documenting one of Enron's scams and the first story ever published that contained proof that California's electricity market was being manipulated.

In May 2002, the Federal Energy Regulatory Commission released internal Enron memos—blueprints—that showed how Enron's traders spent years gaming California's electricity market so they could increase their company's profits. The game that I had written about that Enron played with the transmission lines was called, get this, "Death Star," named after Darth Vader's battle station in *Star Wars*. I felt totally let down when I found out about the code name because I always thought Enron's employees were hip. But they were just a bunch of nerds.

The company memo on "Death Star" says Enron gets paid "for moving energy to relieve congestion without actually moving any energy or relieving any congestion." Basically, what Enron did was clog transmission lines with power they claimed they were selling. Then the state agency that managed the lines paid Enron millions of dollars to divert the electricity to some other part of the power grid because it needed to use that portion of the line. After pulling this scam a few times, Enron figured out that they didn't need to sell any electricity at all. They just threatened to send it over the trans lines, submitting phony documents to prove it, and then they would get paid millions to free up the congestion that was never going to happen in the first place. When the internal Enron memos were released, a copy of the story I wrote on May 3, 2000, was included as background material.

Strange to consider that a scam artist like me was exposing someone else's scams. I felt like Fredo in *The Godfather*, selling out my brother in crime.

I had a hard time understanding all of the fuss surrounding my story when Dale Arden and a few other reporters congratulated me for nailing Enron.

Arden said, "Enron is a hard nut to crack. Unless you have some sort of proof it's hard to write anything negative about them. But you caught them with their hand in the cookie jar. Good scoop."

Arden nominated my story for a Dow Jones ACE award, an honor given to a handful of the best wire stories of the week. I won and got fifty bucks cash. Back in the day, I would have used the money to make myself feel good. But now I was getting high off all the attention. I realize now that the accolades made me feel like I was coming clean about my own past. By pursuing stories about corporate cronyism and shady politicians, I could purge my own feelings of guilt and shame.

A day after my story ran I got a phone call from a senior executive at Southern California Edison, the utility that provides electric service to millions of people in Southern California. The executive said he read my story "with great interest" and wanted to me to continue following it because I would find a lot of "shenanigans going on involving Enron."

"We have a committee here that's spent a year looking into this," the executive said. He insisted on anonymity because he was worried about getting in trouble or losing his job for talking to the media. "We believe Enron has made about fifty million dollars by maliciously overloading the transmission lines and getting paid a fee to relieve it. Enron's not the only one. There are other games being played too by other companies. Look into it. Mark my words, this is going to cause an energy crisis this summer."

No one believed that an energy crisis would hit California. The state's economy was too strong and the dot-com industry—in the heart of California's Silicon Valley—was still thriving. When the energy crisis did hit, it caught everyone in California off guard. Warnings of a looming crisis fell on deaf ears. Politicians simply dismissed them as propaganda. Newspapers barely gave it any play.

Before I had a chance to investigate the tip I got from the Southern California Edison executive, another journalist had already sounded an early alarm about possible electricity shortages and blackouts in California in the summer of 2000.

A week after my story on Enron ran on the wire, Rebecca Smith wrote a front-page story for *The Wall Street Journal* under the headline:

Gloom and Doom: New Rules, Demands Put Dangerous Strain On Electricity Supply

Rebecca's bombshell story was so dead-on accurate in its prediction of what was about to happen that summer, you'd think she was psychic.

Rebecca's story was a perfect example of the journal's influence on corporate America. Her "Gloom and Doom" piece was a sensation on Wall Street and was instrumental in boosting the stock price of a half-dozen energy companies that were seen as the ones that would fill the supply gaps if an electricity shortage did in fact hit California.

There's nothing more demoralizing than being forced to follow up on a competitor's scoop. This feeling of shame sets in when your editor tells you that you have to "match" someone else's scoop with your own version of the story, one you should have reported in the first place because it's on your beat. When Arden told Mark Golden and me to follow up Rebecca's story, I promised myself that I wouldn't be put in that position again. If anyone was going to be forced to follow up a story, my competitors were going to have to play catch-up with me.

I wanted to cozy up to Rebecca Smith, kiss her ass, hoping that we could become friends and maybe work on a story together for the *Journal*. Even though we were competitors, we had the same beat and were both employed by Dow Jones & Co. Although the *Journal* and Dow Jones Newswires are completely autonomous, a Dow Jones reporter could get a byline in the journal if the story was of national importance and somewhat exclusive. Every newswire reporter's goal was to get a byline in the *Journal*, be read by millions of people and, hopefully, one-day make the transition to the paper as a full-time reporter. However, that didn't happen often. Newswire reporters were treated like the journal's unwanted stepchildren. Sort of the way the *Our Times* reporters were treated by the *Los Angeles Times* staff writers.

I found out that Rebecca worked out of the *Journal's* Los Angeles bureau, which was down the hall from my prison cell of an office. Most of the *Journal* reporters I met were egotistical pricks who wouldn't give me the time of day.

I was getting ready to leave the New Jersey office Friday morning to head back to Los Angeles. I had a 6:00 a.m. flight out of Newark. I checked my e-mail one last time and there was a message in my inbox from my old boss, Bill.

"Hey, Jason, this e-mail was sent to Mary Beth (the woman who replaced me as city editor of *Our Times*) and I'm forwarding it to you. I think it's from your father. Why is he yelling?"

My father's e-mail was all in caps. I guess he didn't realize that means you're shouting.

TO WHOM IT MAY CONCERN.

CAN YOU PLEASE TELL WHAT HAPPENED TO JASON LEOPOLD? I HAVEN'T SEEN HIS NAME IN THE PAPER IN A FEW MONTHS.

THANK YOU
STEVE LEOPOLD

I hadn't spoken to my family for nearly three years. They didn't know I went back to rehab or that my marriage nearly fell apart or that I tried to kill myself again. I cut them off three months after Lisa and I were married. I wanted them to take responsibility for screwing up my life, at least part of it. But I couldn't muster up the courage to ask them to. So I just stopped talking to them. My brother and sister said they wouldn't speak with me if I didn't maintain a relationship with my parents, so I cut them off, too.

I decided to respond to my father's e-mail. I felt I was in a good place now. I was twenty-one months sober. For the first time ever, I had a life, a great job, money, a car, an awesome new family, and the best wife in the world.

Dad,

I understand you were looking for me. I got an email from the person at the *Los Angeles Times* who took my position. I am now the Los Angeles bureau chief for Dow Jones Newswires. I guess it would be kind of foolish for me to ask what's up, but what's up? I have been thinking of you and mom and everyone a lot. There have been many times that I wanted to pick up the phone but I felt that so much time has passed. I just didn't know what to say. To be honest, I called the house a couple of times and lost my nerve and hung up. But I was surprised to hear that you got an answering machine. I do hope you are well. Here's my information.

Jason Leopold
Bureau Chief
Dow Jones Newswires
6500 Wilshire Blvd., 15th Floor Los Angeles, CA 90048

I waited. I figured I'd eventually get a response from my father. Ten minutes later it arrived.

Dear Jason:

I just deleted an entire message that I wrote. I guess I was a little emotional hearing from you. I am very happy to hear that you are doing well and you are fine. Jason, I have been monitoring you at the *Los Angeles Times* for quite a while. I know you were the City Editor and I have read some of your articles. Jason, for the life of me I do not understand what happened three months after your wedding. I honestly don't know if in fact you told everyone a bunch of stories or Lisa created this situation or both. I also don't understand your in-laws. I guess that's the Beverly Hills way. I guess we all have issues to cope with. God knows Mommy and I have more than our share. But the situation you created I will never understand. I really don't want to rehash anything. Michelle is pregnant in case you haven't heard. I guess you will be an uncle, hopefully, not an absentee one. Eric is in the process of moving to Florida. By the way, Mommy was watching the wedding channel and saw you on one of the shows. Naturally, she couldn't stop crying. Jason, we all love you and miss you very much. However, due to the circumstances and the situation created, the first move will have to be on your part. It is very easy to email someone, no voice, no face, no emotion. If what you say is sincere, then pick up the telephone and call Mommy, especially that Sunday is MOTHER'S DAY. Jason, you have to come to terms with all that has gone on. As I said, Mommy and I have more grievances than anyone, yet we forgive and forget.

Love,
Dad

He did it again. He succeeded in making me feel guilty for feeling what I have felt for most of my life. He doesn't get it. Never did. He thinks that I can just flick a switch and turn off those images of his fist punching my face or dragging me by my ear through the snow. I couldn't. I thought about it every day. Part of me wanted to take the train to his office on 30th Street, wait for him to walk out, and beat him senseless with a crowbar. The other part of me wanted to see him and give him a hug.

I had a lump in my throat. I felt a bout of depression coming on, so I quickly packed up my stuff and put it into my knapsack and said good-bye to Arden, Mark, and Andrew.

"Looking forward to kicking some serious ass this year," Arden said. "Yeah." Mark said.

"Dude, nice work," Drew added.

I hugged all three of them and left the building. I took the Path train to the World Trade Center and transferred to the Uptown N. I got off at 34th Street, Herald Square. I walked toward 30th Street, to my father's office. He had no idea I was in New York, so I figured I'd surprise him.

My father was packing up a box and taping it shut when I sneaked into his office. He looked older and less intimidating. His hair was thinning and graying and he had a few brown age spots on his forehead, but he still managed to comb his hair back and style it like Elvis circa 1966. For the first time I thought that I could take him on if we got into a fight.

"Hey, Dad," I said.

He turned around and looked right at me. He was clearly shocked. He shook his head as if to say, "I can't believe you're here." I walked toward him and stuck out my hand. He grabbed it, pulled me closer, wrapped his arms around me and held me tight, like he was truly happy to see me.

"You look good," he said.

I was wearing a baby-blue button-down shirt, black slacks, and an expensive tie. My hair was short. I looked conservative, like a banker or a corporate executive.

"Thanks," I said. "I feel good."

We walked down the block to a deli. I got bottled water and a turkey sandwich. My father paid for it. We sat down at a table, and I started to recognize the changes as I looked into my father's eyes. I felt like we'd grown apart, that I really was nothing like him. It was like I was sitting next to a stranger. Dad got right down to business.

"Jason, what happened?"

"You judged me," I said matter-of-factly. "You hit me. I had to do what I had to do to survive."

"I never judged you," he said.

"Yes, you did."

"I gave you ten thousand dollars so your lawyer would keep you out of jail. Is that judging you?

He was right about that. But I knew he couldn't and wouldn't accept responsibility for what he did to me physically or psychologically. As I took a bite out of my turkey sandwich, I realized that these were my issues to deal with, not his. I could easily harbor resentment for him for the rest of my life but doing so seemed pointless. I accepted the fact that he would never change and become the father that I fantasized about. Listening to his denials made me realize that I was the one changing and that I was already a better person because I was willing to accept my father for who he was.

I made a conscious decision to start talking to my parents again. It was a monumental breakthrough for me.

"Look, Dad, let's just agree to disagree and start over."

His eyes teared up. "That's all I ever wanted," he said.

As we walked back to his office, I filled him in on the years of my life he missed, minus my stint in rehab and the drugs that came before it. I didn't want him to know that I had fucked up again. I said goodbye and gave him a hug.

"I'll call Mom on Mother's Day," I said. "I promise." I did.

A few weeks later, on May 22, 2000, an unusual hot spell hit California. Demand for juice to keep residential air conditioners humming outstripped the state's supply and pushed the power grid to the breaking point. The state's grid operator declared one of the first power emergencies in the newly deregulated market, and the utilities, Southern California Edison, San Diego Gas & Electric, and Pacific Gas & Electric, were forced to cut power to some of their large industrial customers, such as manufacturing plants and supermarkets, to keep supply and demand in balance and to prevent the grid from collapsing.

But something else happened that day that was a bit more unusual than the triple-digit temperatures that blanketed the state. A number of power plants were shut down for "routine" maintenance. The energy companies, such as Duke Energy, Reliant Energy, and Williams Cos., which bought the utilities' power plants in order to break up the utilities' monopoly and allow the free market to work under deregulation, claimed that their newly-acquired assets would often break down or "trip" offline because they ran at full capacity and were too old to take such a routine beating. So two things happened that day. Some power plants broke down and some had their prescheduled checkups. That meant that the state was deprived of several thousand megawatts of electricity, just enough power to keep the grid running smoothly. However, with the power plants offline and the supply situation scarce, the wholesale price, which averaged about forty dollars a megawatt-hour, went through the roof. It reached the state-imposed limit of 750 dollars a megawatt-hour and hovered in that range for the next eight months, which helped many energy companies earn a windfall. Consumer advocates and some Democrats in the state Senate and Assembly said this was an orchestrated event, but no one, including me, could find the smoking gun to prove it.

That was the day—May 22, 2000—when the energy crisis started.

It all happened so fast. Up until then, this was really a financial story. But it became a political story and a business story immediately after wholesale electricity prices skyrocketed that day. Consumers' utility bills tripled and they demanded that their local politicians do something about it.

I was thrust into the action, like an eighteen-year-old being drafted into a war, and immediately went to the front lines and reported the story as it unfolded without hesitation. If you wanted to know what was going on with the electricity crisis in California, you had no choice but to read my stories. I was one of only two or three reporters giving the play-by-play.

That week also saw San Diego become the first city in the country to feel the full impact of the newly deregulated electricity market. The results turned out to be disastrous. The city's main utility, San Diego Gas & Electric, was now buying most of its power in the spot market and simply passed the true costs onto its customers. But the promises of cheaper electricity as a result of competition in California had the opposite effect. Consumers' utility bills soared because sellers had the power to name their price. A public outcry ensued. A blackout rolled through San Francisco and Governor Davis ordered state regulators to investigate the nature behind the outage and the price swings in San Diego.

The California Independent System Operator (CAISO), the state agency that kept the grid in check and managed supply and demand, provided temporary relief to the price spikes in the form of a bandage. The CAISO's governing board had the authority to lower the state-mandated price cap—the maximum price sellers can charge—on electricity sold in California, which the CAISO did, twice, from 750 dollars a megawatt-hour to $500/Mwh and finally to $250/Mwh. But that only made the situation worse. Other states in the West were also saddled with a power shortage, and they were willing to outbid the $250/

Mwh cap that California's grid operator maintained. So most of the energy companies essentially told California to fuck off and sold their supplies to Oregon, Arizona, Washington, and other Western states for top dollar, leaving California so short of power that the state faced the prospect of rolling blackouts for the first time since World War II.

Here's the crucial mistake the CAISO made that exacerbated the energy crisis: By refusing to allow the rate to exceed the $250/Mwh price cap, the state was left with a massive power shortage. The CAISO, whose main function was to keep the lights on no matter what, found itself forced in turn to buy supplies—those it had initially refused from the energy companies—from the other Western states, at prices that far exceeded its own $250/Mwh cap. It didn't take long before the energy companies realized they could make a fortune by bypassing California's price cap, selling their power to, say, Arizona, and creating an artificial shortage in California, then letting the market boost the price and reselling the same power back to California for as much as $1,500/Mwh. In one week in May 2000, California spent 850 million dollars to keep the lights on. A year before, it cost about ninety million dollars.

There was nothing illegal, per se, about this scam, known in the industry as "ping-pong," which I was lucky enough to be the first one to expose on September 26, 2000. But it would be one of the pieces of evidence used by federal investigators three years later to show how California's power market was manipulated by some rogue Enron traders who masterminded the scheme.

So here I am, knee-deep in the biggest story of the new millennium, trying to figure out how the hell it happened, what in God's name it meant, and how and when it was going to be fixed. I'm fucking obsessed with this story. I can't sleep, I can't eat, and I can't bear to leave the office at a decent hour because of the possibility that news will break and I won't be around to report it. Everybody is blaming everyone else for the crisis and no one has any idea how to solve it. The utilities are pointing fingers at the energy companies, claiming they rigged the market; the energy companies are blaming the utilities, saying they're not buying power in advance, when the price is low; the Democrats are blaming former Governor Pete Wilson, a Republican who signed deregulation into law; and the Wall Street analysts are blaming state officials for allowing the crisis to spiral out of control. So I start to phone every fucking PR person at all the major energy companies to ask them what can be done.

"Gotta get the utilities to sign long-term contracts," Tom Williams, the PR guy at Duke Energy, told me in July 2000. "If they sign some long-term deals they can get a fixed price and they won't have to rely on buying all of their power in the spot market."

Tom told me that his company made an offer to SDG&E to sell the company most of its power needs for about five-and-a-half cents per kilowatt-hour, roughly ten times less than SDG&E was paying in the spot market, but SDG&E turned down the offer. California regulators had prohibited the utilities from signing long-term deals with energy companies—a crucial mistake that would cost the state tens of billions of dollars—but I wrote up the story anyway. It was clear that the market, as it was designed, wasn't working and the rules needed to change.

I felt that this would also be a good time to approach Rebecca Smith about teaming up to write a story together. A meeting was scheduled to take place in San Diego in mid-July 2000 with executives from SDG&E, consumer groups, and state and local officials about possible remedies to the sky-high wholesale power prices that were crippling small businesses in the city and forcing some low income residents to decide whether to pay their power bill or buy food. The meeting was closed to the public, so I figured I could get Rebecca to take a ride with me to San Diego and protest the media blackout—that maybe we could split up, find out what happened at the meeting, and share a byline.

I walked into the *Journal* newsroom where Rebecca was writing a story. Rebecca was in her early forties, with short dark hair, glasses, and a distinctly asexual presence. Her head was shaped like a perfect square. She could have been Herman Munster's sister, and she even had bangs that looked glued to her forehead. Still, being in her presence was intimidating. She had an aura of being very intellectual. It always seemed she was right about everything, and everyone else was wrong.

"Hey, Rebecca," I said.

"Hi," she said, swiveling her head around for a second to greet me and then back to work.

"So, what do you think about this meeting in San Diego?" I asked. "I was thinking we should go down there together and demand they open it up to the media."

"Yeah, I may be interested in that," she said, still typing.

"Whadda ya think about, I dunno, maybe, ya know, sharing some info, doing a story together…"

She stopped typing and turned her chair around and looked at me. It was the kind of look that didn't require words to express what it was that she was thinking.

"You know, I got a problem with that story you wrote today," she said.

"Which one?" I asked.

"The one about Duke offering San Diego a five-and-a-half cent deal to manage its portfolio," she said. "It's wrong."

"Why is it wrong?" I asked, defensively. "I spoke to Duke. There's nothing wrong with that story."

"Yes there is," she said. "State law says the utilities can't sign long-term contracts so it doesn't matter what offer Duke puts on the table. Your story is pointless."

"So who cares about the law? I reported what Duke offered 'em. I'm just trying to show that someone's got a solution. I dunno, maybe they'll change the rules."

"They can't change the rules," she said. "They'd have to amend the legislation and that'll never happen."

"How do you know?" I asked.

"Oh, go on," she said, throwing up her hands. "Go write what you want."

I lost it.

"HEY!" I said, my voice reaching a pitch that attracted the attention of the other journal reporters. "Don't you dare toss your hands up at me! Who the hell do you think you are? I'm doing my job. I'm reporting the news. You got a problem with that, you can take it up with my editor. But don't you ever toss your hands up at me or criticize my reporting. Understood?"

I marched out of the *Journal* newsroom huffing and puffing. Rebecca seemed to push all of my insecurity buttons and made me doubt the accuracy of my reporting.

A couple of minutes later, Rebecca came looking for me. She poked her head into my office and called out my name.

"What do you want?" I said.

She walked back to my cubicle, pulled up a chair, and sat down next to me. She apologized for throwing her hands up in my face but said she had been getting a lot of phone calls since I started covering the electricity beat, about numerous inaccuracies in my stories.

"What stories?" I asked, scrolling through the hundreds of reports I'd written on electricity over the past three months. "Why are you getting phone calls? Why hasn't anyone called me?"

"Well, I'm not sure," she said. "But you know I'm the expert here on AB1890. Everyone knows that. I've been writing about this since 1996. I'm also older than you and have a lot more experience. You're just starting out."

"Uh, sorry, Rebecca, I'm not just starting out," I said. "I've been reporting for more than four years."

"Well, you're just starting out on this beat and it's a very complicated topic," she said. "You're bound to make errors."

I challenged her to look at my stories and point out the errors, but she resisted. She got up to leave and said maybe, when we're both not so consumed with work, we could take a break and have lunch together. That day would never come.

My competitive side took over and my perceptions of Rebecca became irrational. I made it my mission to steal her thunder, to scoop the shit out of her, make her look bad, and force her to follow up on my reports until she was fired. Then I would take over her job, I imagined. I became so caught up with resentment that the only thing I could think of when I wrote a story was the look on her face when she read it.

By August 2000, the energy crisis had made national headlines. Power prices continued to skyrocket, shortages persisted, and power emergencies had become routine. Out-of-state energy companies, such as Enron, Duke, Dynegy, Williams, Reliant, and Mirant, were taking a verbal beating by Democrats in the state legislature who accused the companies of gouging

Californians. I didn't buy it. For one, the politicians had no evidence to back up their claims and, two, it was well-known that it was more than a decade since any new power plants were built in California. So, while demand surged, supplies remained stagnant. Plus, the summer of 2000 was one of the hottest on record. Anyone who had an air conditioner didn't think twice about using it, and that sucked up most of the state's juice.

That said, the slant to Dow Jones' coverage of the energy crisis was definitely in favor of the energy companies, despite the fact that many of the price-gouging and manipulation claims against the power companies turned out to be true. But I for one didn't think for a second that the CEOs, the Wall Street analysts, and the other energy company executives I interviewed on a daily basis were lying through their teeth when they told me that they were being unfairly penalized by the state and that they never, ever, engaged in market manipulation. I bought their line of bullshit and so did a dozen or so other journalists who covered the crisis.

But back in the summer of 2000, I believed it was the politicians who were fucking things up with their knee-jerk reactions, their threats of lawsuits, and intimidation tactics like threatening to seize the energy companies' power plants through eminent domain. *This is a state government with way too much power*, I thought, *and it's time to expose some politicians and their bullshit.*

My first victim was State Senator Stephen Peace, a Democrat from San Diego whose constituents wanted the blood of SDG&E and anyone else responsible for doubling and tripling their monthly power bills.

Peace was best known for writing and starring in the 1978 cult movie *Attack of the Killer Tomatoes!* a film, ironically, about the government's incompetent handling of an unexpected crisis (i.e., killer tomatoes' murderous spree in San Diego). In the film's climactic ending, Peace's character leads the people of San Diego in stomping out the vegetable menace in a football stadium. Peace must have been watching the cult classic again when he decided to lead hundreds of San Diegans to the offices of SDG&E in early August 2000 to burn their electricity bills.

But few people realized at the time that Peace was the architect of AB1890, the state's landmark deregulation law. Peace was the one who locked other legislators in a conference room during a two-week marathon session in 1996 to work out the kinks of AB1890 and to ensure everyone—utilities, energy companies, unions—got what they wanted. Then he forced the bill down everyone's throat on the last day the legislature was in session during the summer of 1996. Those sessions became known in legislative circles as the "Steve Peace Death March."

Now, Peace was fucked. His name was all over AB1890. The energy crisis, which was due in part to regulatory restrictions that Peace left in place in the legislation, could end his political career if people were reminded just how big a role he played in electricity deregulation, which is what I set out to do in a series of scathing articles.

Peace tried to distance himself from the bill that he sponsored, going as far as demanding the state return to a regulated market and producing a public service announcement on his website saying it was a "myth" that he was the architect of deregulation.

"I'm not a supporter of competition," Peace said in the video, highlighting one of eight so-called myths about him and deregulation, "I'm in favor of maintaining a regulated environment."

He made himself an easy target. I dug through some older news stories where Peace is quoted as championing deregulation, copied down the quotes, and wrote a story exposing him speaking out of both sides of his mouth. He never recovered from the beating he took in the press and his aspirations to become California's Secretary of State never got off the ground. That's a great thing about being a journalist.

August 2000 turned out to be a good month for me. I won a few ACE awards, dozens of sources were warming up to me, and I was tapped to appear on CNBC, cable's business channel, also partially owned by Dow Jones, as an expert to talk about the energy crisis. "Whadda ya think about that, Rebecca?" I said to myself.

My editor, Arden Dale, and her boss, Neal Lipschutz, sent out a note to all of Dow Jones saying, "Jason has been at ground zero of California's massive power problems, staying ahead on all the important market-related news about the state's electricity woes."

My ego was getting bigger. There was certainly no shortage of kudos at Dow Jones. If you were good, everyone knew about it. I used that note to hustle Arden for more money. I told her that I had been approached by several other news organizations that wanted to hire me away and pay me more money to cover the energy crisis for them, a story that was entirely untrue. She said there was no way she'd let me go. She offered me a 5,000-dollar raise and a 5,000 dollar year-end bonus. I accepted.

It occurred to me an hour before I was scheduled to go live on CNBC that I could be exposed as a convicted felon if there was someone out there who knew about my past, saw me on television, and decided to rat me out to Arden or Andrew. I had an anxiety attack and went into the bathroom to throw up.

I called Lisa to tell her about the show, but she said she was too nervous to watch me live—what if I fucked up right there on national television? She wouldn't know what to do or how to help me, she said.

I stared at my reflection in the mirror. I didn't look like a felon. I cleaned myself up and said fuck it. I had already put myself out there. If someone wanted to expose me, they would have done it by now. I wasn't going to back down. This was the big break I'd been waiting for: a chance to prove to the world that I had made it.

I walked into the journal newsroom. That's where CNBC's remote camera was located. All I had to do was sit in the chair, stick the earpiece in my ear, and wait for Ron Insana, a CNBC anchor, to shoot me some questions about the energy crisis.

"And we're going live in five, four, three...I'm Ron Insana. California was the first state in the nation to deregulate electricity. Consumers and businesses were promised they'd see lower bills and reliable service. But this summer, the state is facing a massive shortage, the prospect of blackouts, and price spikes. Here to explain how it all happened is Dow Jones Newswires Los Angeles bureau chief Jason Leopold. Welcome Jason."

I stumbled a bit, used "um" and "you know" too many times. But the CNBC producer, Sean Bender, who, ironically, used to have Arden's job some years back, said I did a pretty good job considering it was my first time on live TV.

I waited for the shit to fall.

The CNBC appearance led to dozens of invitations to discuss what it was like to cover the "first big story of the new millennium." I also did numerous radio interviews on National Public Radio, and my scoops were being cited in newspapers like the *San Diego Union Tribune* and the *San Francisco Chronicle*. Sean invited me back onto CNBC ten more times. The *Journal's* Los Angeles bureau chief, Jonathan Friedland, thought Rebecca was the better choice and called Sean to tell him that.

After that it became clear, at least in my mind, that Friedland didn't like me one bit. The only reason I could think of was that I was scooping him and Rebecca over and over and over again. I did an interview with Warren Olney, host of the popular NPR program "Which Way L.A." Olney identified me as a *The Wall Street Journal* reporter, but I let it go without comment. The next morning Friedland sent me an e-mail objecting to the fact that Olney identified me as a *Journal* reporter. He told me not to let it happen again.

I shot him back an e-mail that must have made his blood boil. "Oh well! Too late," I wrote, and included a smiley face in the body of the text.

In September, the Federal Energy Regulatory Commission, the agency that oversees interstate energy markets, caved in to political pressure and launched an investigation into the power crisis-specifically, whether energy companies were manipulating the market. California was demanding some three billion dollars in refunds for alleged overcharges, and the uncertainty surrounding the outcome of the investigation depressed the stock price of nearly every energy company that did business in California.

Governor Davis, who did a miserable job of dealing with the crisis—choosing instead to publicly spew venom at a select group of Texas energy corporations, such as Reliant, Enron, and Dynegy, who he said were ripping off the state—carried on about FERC failing to do its job to keep power prices at "just and reasonable" levels. The FERC commissioners, most of whom were free-market conservatives, didn't appreciate Davis politicizing the crisis. One commissioner in particular hated him with venom.

That gave me an idea. In late October, a couple of weeks before FERC was going to release the findings of their investigation, I called that commissioner and told him that I wanted to be his source for everything that came down the pike that had to do with the governor's response to the energy crisis. I said to the commissioner, "You need to know what's going on. A lot of mud is being thrown in your direction. I'm pro-deregulation, like you. We can't let these bastards pull the plug. I want you to know what's going on behind the scenes in Sacramento so you can respond accordingly before it's public knowledge." I also let the commissioner know that, like him, I was a staunch Republican (a lie) and we needed to stick together.

The problem with that, however, was that the governor's office wasn't interested in sharing their plans, if in fact they had any, with the media. Davis was notorious for his secrecy on political issues and his press dog Maviglio wouldn't give up any information when I pressed him.

So I called up the commissioner two days later and told him I had had an interview with the governor and that I wanted to give him the details of our conversation before I wrote a story about it.

"Wait," the commissioner said, "Call me on my cell phone. Don't say anything on this line."

I called him back on his cell phone and made up a wild tale about how Davis told me he had the details of FERC's investigation, and that he told me that FERC was going to order refunds and the energy companies were culpable for manipulating the market.

"I can't believe you guys caved," I said, emphasizing how disappointed I was. "I wanted you to know what the governor said before I put my story on the wire."

The commissioner was infuriated. He just let loose.

"That son of a bitch," he said. "Goddamnit! Boy, is he going to be in for a rude awakening. I don't know where the governor got his information but it's flat-out wrong."

My devious plan worked. I knew that if I could make the commissioner think that Davis believed he was going to win this fight, and was communicating that to the media, I could get the commissioner fired up enough to leak details of the investigation, and as a result, I would have one of the biggest exclusives in the country. I hesitate to admit it, but I get pleasure out of striking a match, starting a blaze, and watching it burn. My story was going to be a fucking inferno.

"Well, we can't let Davis get away with this," I told the commissioner. "He's lying! He's probably trying to get the media to say that there will be refunds to put pressure on you."

"You're probably right," the commissioner said, "but we won't cave in to political pressure."

"Can you give me the lowdown?"

The commissioner said he couldn't give me any details of the investigation because that would violate federal law about discussing pending investigations.

"I got an idea," I said. "I'll ask you if you have any problem with what I'm going to write. That way you won't actually be giving me any details. Obviously, I'll keep your name totally out of it."

"Give it a shot," the commissioner said. "Let me see what you mean."

"If I was going to write a story saying that FERC won't order generators to pay refunds to California, would you have a problem with that?"

"No. I wouldn't have a problem with that at all."

That was the most important part of the investigation because the energy companies could have been forced to return the summer windfall profits they made as a result of the price spikes, which would have caused their stocks to nosedive.

"If I were to write that energy companies didn't manipulate the market, would you have a problem with that?"

"Nope."

"How about if I said that California was mostly to blame for the crisis because the state wouldn't allow utilities to sign long-term contracts and that it left too many regulatory restrictions in place, would that be a problem for you?"

"Not at all."

I thanked him and hung up the phone. I felt like I snorted up a line of coke the size of a Texas caterpillar. I called Andrew to tell him I got a breaking story that needed to get on the wire.

"Dude, drop everything you're doing," I said. "Got the details of the FERC investigation."

"What? Holy shit, dude! How'd you score that one?"

"The FERC commissioner gave me all the details."

"Who was it?"

I told Andrew which commissioner it was; he knew after I revealed the source's identity that he had given me accurate information because he was also a reliable source for other Dow Jones stories. I didn't tell Andrew how I manipulated the commissioner; I was afraid he'd kill the story.

The market was going to close in thirty minutes and we wanted to get the story out before the closing bell, so we started flashing headlines across the wire first, which alerted Wall Street that news was breaking.

The first headline went out on October 27, 2000, at about 3:30 p.m.

FERC Finds No Abuse of Calif Elec Market— Commissioner

Another headline was sent out a couple of seconds later.

FERC Won't Order Generators To Pay Calif Refunds—Commissioner

After you send headlines out on the wire you have fifteen minutes to send the first three grafs of the story onto the wire. My phone wouldn't stop ringing. Everyone on Wall Street, analysts and traders and bankers and even the energy companies being investigated by FERC, already knew I was the one who broke the news. They didn't want to wait for the story. They were too impatient. They wanted to speak directly with me. But I let my phone ring into voicemail.

This was the biggest story of my career at Dow Jones and it made a huge impact, bigger than Rebecca's front-page story for the *Journal* five months earlier. My story actually moved the market. The Dow Jones Industrial Average moved up a point or two because the uncertainty surrounding the energy sector was removed, now that FERC determined that energy companies wouldn't have to refund the state, and traders started buying up as much stock in Enron, Dynegy, Reliant, and Williams, to name a few, as fast as they could. If you look at those energy companies' stock charts, you would see a blip a second or two after my story hit the wire.

My phone was still ringing. I was nervous as hell that if there were anything wrong with this story, I would lose my job and my career would be over. This wasn't some local story about a kid getting killed in a tae kwon do tournament; this was national news and a major blow to California, particularly to

Governor Davis. My entire story was based on a conversation with an anonymous commissioner. All of the major newspapers in the country were going to scrutinize it. In a matter of minutes I went from financial reporter to national political reporter, and the journalists that usually cover that beat were going to want to know who Jason Leopold was, why he was treading on their turf, and how he got his sources to leak him the details of the power probe. I didn't want to answer the phone, but the ringing was driving me nuts.

"This is Jason."

"Jason Leopold?" the woman on the other end of the phone asked.

"Yes. This is he."

"I have Jeff Skilling on the line for you."

Jeff Skilling was the president of Enron and the brain behind the company's electricity trading operation. I didn't know much about him at the time, other than he was the one who lobbied California officials in 1994 and said deregulation would save the state nine billion dollars—money that could go to education, he said. I interviewed him a couple of times during the crisis. Mark Palmer set up those interviews. But this call was unexpected.

"Okay. Thanks."

"Go ahead," the woman said.

"It's Jeff Skilling. I just read your story, Jason. Fantastic piece of work!"

"Thanks," I said. "I really appreciate that."

"As far as I can tell you're the only one who has the story," Skilling said.

"Yeah. It's definitely exclusive."

"Can I ask you which commissioner leaked you the report?"

"I can't say," I said. "I'm sorry."

"Is he reliable?"

"Totally," I said. "This is 100 percent on the money."

"Great. That's just great. I wish I could see the look on Governor Davis' face when he gets the news."

"Yeah. Me too."

"Okay. Good work, Jason. Keep it up."

I got similar calls from executives at Dynegy, Mirant, Reliant, and Duke and from analysts and traders. They all wanted to make sure the story was bulletproof. I felt omnipotent. I was in love with this power. I was unstoppable. I needed to stay high.

I also got a call from Steve Maviglio. I hadn't spoken to him much before this story came out, but he asked me to keep in touch with him because he could give me a comment on behalf of the governor if I were to write another story like this. He gave me his cell phone number. That was the start of our relationship. In less than a month, I started leaking him information that consumer groups, energy companies, FERC, and Republican legislators were going to use as ammunition against the governor in exchange for an exclusive here and there. But I also leaked the information Maviglio gave me to the other side in exchange for exclusives from them. I was obsessed, self-absorbed, and narcissistic. I didn't care about ethics. In fact, I didn't even think about ethical violations. I just wanted to be the first one to get to the truth.

No one was able to match my story, and it put me on the map. Several major newspapers cited it and I was interviewed by NPR and appeared on CNBC again.

A couple of weeks after I broke the story on the FERC probe, the commission convened a meeting in Washington, DC, and released the findings of their investigation. But before they did, a couple of commissioners criticized the lone commissioner who leaked the report to me. No one knew the identity of my source, but the commissioners said if they found out they would demand that he or she would face criminal charges. Senator Steve Peace was at the meeting and also chimed in.

"I don't know why you're bothering telling us the outcome of your investigation," he said. "We already know about it thanks to Jason Leopold."

When the FERC released their report, it confirmed every element of my story. That was a huge weight off of my shoulders. Arden called me to say that one of the editors of the *Journal* called her, telling her they would have picked up my story—but that when the editor had called Jonathan Friedland to inquire about it, he said that I was untrustworthy and there was a strong chance the story, when it broke, was wrong.

I was fucking livid. I walked into Friedland's office and slammed the door shut.

"What's your fucking problem?" I asked.

"What are you talking about?" Friedland said.

"I just got off the phone with my editor," I said. "She told me you told Marcus Brauchli that I'm untrustworthy, that my FERC story was wrong. Did you listen to the FERC hearing? My story was dead-on. Where do you get off trying to sabotage me?"

"I'm sorry," Friedland said, which I didn't expect to hear from him.

"Yeah? You ever have a problem with a story I write, you come to me," I said. "It's not my problem that I'm slaughtering your reporter on this beat. But don't talk shit about me."

This is a cutthroat business. No matter how good you are, or think you are, there's always someone who'll try to drag you down. Everyone was talking shit about me. My competitors hated me, or so I was told, because their editors forced them to follow up my stories, and no matter how hard I worked I couldn't win the respect of the editors at the *Journal*. But sometimes being aggressive has its rewards.

When Arden called me later that month she sounded out of breath, like she just finished running a marathon.

"Jason...got...good...news." she said, panting. "You won!"

"Arden, I don't understand what you're trying to say."

"Hang...on," she said. "You won! You won the Dow Jones Newswires award. Journalist of the year!"

I knew Arden nominated me for the award, an honor bestowed upon Dow Jones' top six journalists worldwide, for my coverage of the energy crisis. But I never thought I'd win. I was insecure about the veracity of my own reporting because I used anonymous sources in some of my stories and competitors attacked me for it. News organizations like *Bloomberg* wouldn't even bother reporting a story unless they had someone on the record to back it up. Very few of my sources would allow me to use their names because they were frightened about the repercussions. I guessed the awards judges, who worked at the Associated Press, *Barron's*, and the *Journal*, would frown upon that. But my stories always held up. I got a 5,000-dollar cash prize and a trophy.

I continued to plug away. The energy crisis showed no signs of calming down. Prices continued to spike. Southern California Edison and Pacific Gas & Electric started to bleed cash; the prices they paid for electricity were higher than the amount they were legally allowed to charge customers. By late December 2000, both utilities teetered on the brink of bankruptcy. The energy companies refused to sell the utilities power because the utilities couldn't afford to pay for it. By January 2001, the energy companies withheld power from the state due to the utilities' deteriorating financial situation, and California suffered through three consecutive days of rolling blackouts.

On April 6, 2001, less than twenty-four hours after Governor Davis took the unusual step of addressing the state live on radio and television and refused to raise electricity rates to keep SoCal Ed and PG&E solvent, PG&E filed for Chapter 11 bankruptcy protection. It looked like the company's way of saying "fuck you" to Davis.

I was devastated by the bankruptcy news. I was in my car and my colleague Jessica called me on my cell phone and let me down gently. She knew I had been working on that story for months, begging sources at the company to phone me the moment they filed bankruptcy papers. I was convinced I was going to be the first one to break the news.

It turns out that I missed the story because I was in Santa Monica meeting my probation officer for the last time. That was the week I completed my five-year stint and finished paying off three grand in restitution. My probation officer gave me a clean bill of health and sent me on my way.

"Good luck," he said. "Stay outta trouble."

I made up for missing the PG&E bankruptcy story six months later.

On October 3, 2001, I got lucky again. I broke the news that Southern California Edison had reached a controversial deal with state regulators allowing the utility to pay off its three billion dollar debt and avoid bankruptcy. I got the story from a high-ranking executive at the utility about an hour before state regulators made an official announcement. Andrew sent out an e-mail to the Dow Jones top brass saying I beat our closest competitors, Reuters and *Bloomberg*, by a long shot. The story in and of itself was an important one because it signified the end to the nearly two-year energy crisis and proved that Dow Jones Newswires led the coverage of the whole debacle.

Gil Alexander, spokesman for SoCal Ed, sent me a congratulatory e-mail. "I want you to know, Jason, that your work is the buzz of our senior people," Gil's note said. "You were first with the story. They don't know how you get stories so quickly but they think there is no one like you in that regard."

Not quickly enough. Two weeks later, Rebecca Smith and her colleague John Emshwiller broke the news exposing Enron as a house of cards. That's when things started to go terribly wrong.

TEN

I DIDN'T SEE IT COMING. I thought Rebecca Smith couldn't
compete with me but she was onto something bigger. She
was investigating Enron the whole time.

I'm not sure who I resented more when the Enron scandal
was first exposed on October 16, 2001—Rebecca for nailing the
story or Mark Palmer at Enron for spending over a year stroking
my ego and convincing me that neither Enron nor any other
energy company was manipulating the California power market.

For twenty-four days, Rebecca and John Emshwiller
hammered away at Enron with a series of exclusive, biting
stories that uncovered how the company cooked its books. They
destroyed Enron with their exposé. It was the biggest scandal to
hit corporate America and it made both of them stars.

I was enraged at being overshadowed by Rebecca and John
and losing the attention of editors and colleagues. Something
inside snapped. I lost it and fell right back into my drug addict
ways of thinking.

I became totally consumed and obsessed with Enron and
with beating Rebecca and John to the punch by uncovering
more instances of fraud at the firm.

Because Enron's downfall had huge implications for the
future of deregulation and the electricity market in general, I

was allowed to pursue the Enron story from whatever angle I chose. But there was no way I could compete with Rebecca and John. Every day, they published a new revelation about Enron. What did they have that I didn't?

I called Mark Palmer, convinced that he was Rebecca and John's source.

"Mark, it's Jason," I said. I would have loved to give him a verbal beating right then for manipulating me when I was covering the energy crisis, having me focus exclusively on the state government's role, but deep down I knew it was my fault for trusting him.

"How the fuck are Rebecca and John pulling this off?" I asked. "I want a taste, too. Can you hook me up with some info, puh-leeez?"

"I don't have anything for you, Jason," Mark said. "Someone sent Rebecca and John a box of documents. That's how they've been getting all of these stories."

My criminal mind briefly took over, and I seriously considered stealing Rebecca and John's material. I stayed at the office until ten one night and snuck into the journal office. I had a key, given to me after I made an appearance on CNBC one morning, before anybody at the journal reported for work, and had to get security to open the door for me.

No one was inside the journal newsroom. It was pretty dark except for the fluorescent glow that beamed off the computer monitors. My heart started racing. What stopped me from looking for the documents was that I knew I could do my own digging. I didn't need their fucking documents. I kicked ass on the energy crisis. Why should Enron be any different?

I left and went home. I started cruising Internet chat rooms. That's where a couple of *Journal* reporters hung out in 2000 and found out about the AM/Time Warner merger. Apparently some executives of both companies were talking about it in code and the *Journal* reporters figured it out. I thought, *Hey, who knows, maybe I'll get lucky and Ken Lay or someone will brag about looting the company.*

I typed Andrew Fastow's name into the Yahoo! message board to see what would come up. Fastow was Enron's chief financial officer and allegedly the brains behind the corruption. I needed an in, something I could use to get him to talk to me. Fastow's name was plastered all over the Yahoo! message board. There were death threats made against him by people whose investments in Enron sank when the company's stock went into the toilet. Fastow's home phone number and directions to his house were posted on the message board.

"Die Fastow, die," one of the messages said.

I took a personal interest in Fastow when I got to a page on Yahoo! that contained hundreds of anti-Semitic postings blaming Enron's downfall on "Fastow, the dirty filthy Jew." "Kike kills Enron," and "Jews are ruining our country" were just some of the statements anonymous people had posted. Had any of these people posted their real names, I would have dug up their phone numbers and threatened to kill them. Suddenly I had empathy for Fastow. I also felt that Fastow and I shared a common bond, not just as Jews but as criminals. Fastow looted Enron and I looted Milan.

The anti-Semitic postings were my in to Fastow, as I planned to write a story about the hate speech against him. I used my Jewish blood as a way to get the first comments the embattled chief financial officer made to the media since Enron collapsed.

I called Fastow at home on December 4, 2001, and left him a message.

"Mr. Fastow, this is Jason Leopold," I said, "I'm the bureau chief of Dow Jones Newswires. I want to write a story about these anti-Semitic postings on the Internet. I want you to know that I'm also Jewish. My grandparents are Holocaust survivors. I went to Yeshiva when I was a kid. I have a personal interest in seeing these messages removed from the Internet. It's wrong and I'm offended by it."

Fastow's criminal attorney, David Gerger, called me from Houston a few hours after I left Fastow a voicemail. He said Fastow gave him permission to speak on his behalf.

"I'm also Jewish, Mr. Leopold," Gerger said. "I too find these anti-Semitic statements reprehensible."

Gerger told me that the Houston police were aware of the threats and were keeping an eye on Fastow and his family. I used the opportunity to ask Gerger what role Fastow played in Enron's fall. Much to my surprise he responded to my question. No other journalists, not even Rebecca and John, had so far been able to get Fastow or his attorneys to comment on that. This was my first exclusive on the Enron scandal.

"Andy Fastow is not the cause of Enron's losses," Gerger told me. "Unfortunately, people look for scapegoats and in this case it would be very wrong to scapegoat Andy Fastow. The factual picture is Andy did what Enron authorized."

I hung up the phone with Gerger and called Yahoo! I told the spokeswoman about the anti-Semitic postings. She said she was unaware of it, but said it violated the company's policy and Yahoo! immediately wiped them off the message boards. I called Gerger back and told him the news. "Fantastic!" he said. "Andy will be so happy."

On December 4, 2001, the headline, "Ex-CFO Fastow Didn't Cause Enron's Collapse, Lawyer Says," ran across the newswire.

Although my intention was to highlight the anti-Semitism Fastow had endured as a result of his accounting trickery, my editors felt that we should downplay that part of the story and write it around Gerger's on-the-record statements exonerating Fastow, making Dow Jones the first news outlet to print a story that had someone directly connected to Fastow commenting about his ties to the financial fraud.

I used the Fastow story to get to Jeffrey Skilling. Skilling abruptly resigned from Enron two months before Rebecca and John first exposed the fraud. Skilling said he left Enron for personal reasons, but once the company crumbled everyone believed he knew some shit was eventually gonna go down.

Many journalists were curious to find out what Skilling knew about Enron and when he knew it. He was inundated with interview requests, and he wasn't talking. I cold-called Skilling's spokesman Denis Calabrese and told him about my interview with Fastow's attorney. I invented details, as I did a year earlier when I got the FERC commissioner to leak details of the commission's probe into California's power market, and told Calabrese that David Gerger told me off the record that Skilling knew that Fastow was lining his own pockets.

"Gerger says Skilling was in the know," I told Calabrese. "He said the board approved everything Fastow did and Skilling was on the board. I just want you to know what's being said so you're not caught off guard if Fastow starts to sing."

Calabrese bought it. I called Gerger and planned on telling him about a made-up conversation I had with Skilling's people who told me off the record that he had no idea what Fastow was doing. Gerger put me in touch with Fastow's spokesman, Gordon Andrew, in New Jersey. I bullshitted him, too. I was hoping to get both sides so paranoid that one was going to implicate the other—and that either Skilling or Fastow or both would agree to give me an exclusive interview to set the record straight. I sent Calabrese documents on Enron that Andrew had sent me and Andrew documents that Calabrese had sent me. I led each camp to believe that I was its inside source and the only journalist willing to vindicate either of them if they spoke to me exclusively. Truth is, Skilling and Fastow could have stubbed their big toes and it would have been front-page news. Other than Osama bin Laden, Skilling, and Fastow were the most sought-after interview subjects in the world. It didn't matter what either of them said just as long as they said something on the record.

I kept the charade going for three weeks. Calabrese and Andrew were running around in circles, like dogs chasing their tails, trying to figure out how to respond to the bullshit I flung at them. Calabrese caved first. He called me on Wednesday, December 19, at about six in the evening.

"Jason?"

"Yeah?"

"It's Denis Calabrese. Skilling's attorneys are really appreciative that you've been keeping us in the loop on Fastow."

"No problem. Like I said, I genuinely like Skilling and I hate to see him get blamed for all of this."

"Well, your good deeds are gonna pay off," Calabrese said. "Skilling is going to do some interviews. You're one of three people who gets to talk to him."

I froze for a second or two. It was so surreal. Right then I knew I had just landed the biggest story of my career. The first thing that popped into my head was Rebecca Smith. I prayed that she wasn't one of the other two chosen to interview Skilling.

"Denis, this is fucking unbelievable," I said. "I need to ask, though, who are the other two people interviewing him? I probably won't be able to do this if the *Journal's* also doing it."

"We didn't ask the *Journal*," Denis said. "Skilling's pretty angry at them for beating up on the company. It's gonna be the *Houston Chronicle*, because it's his hometown paper, *The New York Times*, and you."

Fucking A. I could scoop the papers. The *Times* and the *Chronicle* would be a day behind me because I could get my story onto the wire the same day I wrote it. There's no way the *Journal* could ignore this one.

"When is this gonna happen?" I asked.

"Well, that's the only drawback," Calabrese said. "You'd have to be in Washington, DC, by Friday at noon. So let's see, you're on the West Coast, I guess that means you'd have to leave tomorrow night."

"I'll be there," I said. "Where is this gonna take place?"

"At O'Melveney and Meyers," Calabrese said. "Bruce Hiler is Skilling's attorney. He's going to represent Skilling when he meets with Congress and the SEC. I won't be there. But I'll give Bruce your information and I'll send you an e-mail with directions to the law office."

"Perfect." I said. "One favor, though. Can you try not to let this get out to anyone? If the *Journal* finds out I'm doing this interview, they may try to steal it from me."

"We're keeping a tight lid on it," he said. "Don't worry."

I let out a loud scream after I hung up the phone.

"What? What happened?" asked Jessica, the other energy reporter, who was still in the office.

"I just fucking scored an interview with Jeff Skilling!"

"Holy shit!" she said, "Are you fucking serious?"

I still needed permission to fly to DC and do the interview. The flight was going to cost a bundle because I could only give the airline a day's notice. The cheapest flight was three thousand dollars. I called Andrew Dowell at home at 11:00 p.m. East Coast time.

"Drew, this is huge," I said. "I just scored an interview with Skilling. But I have to fly to DC to do it. The interview is noon Friday."

"All right, I'll call Gene," he said. "Where are you? I'll call you back."

"At the office."

Gene Colter was deputy managing editor of the Dow Jones Newswires. When Drew called me back he said that Gene wanted to know if the *Journal* was doing the interview, too.

"No," I said. "It's just *The New York Times*, the *Houston Chronicle*, and me."

"Okay," Drew said. "The other thing Gene wanted to know is if you would consider letting someone from this office do the interview 'cause it would be cheaper to get to DC from Jersey."

"Are you out of your fucking mind? Do you know what I had to do to get this interview? I worked on this for more than a fucking month. No way am I gonna let this get away. Fuck that."

"Calm down," Drew said.

If Drew had shot me down, I would have quit right on the spot. I would have flown to DC on my own dime and sold the interview to another magazine or newspaper. Lucky for Drew he gave me the green light.

"Dude, whatever you do, don't let too many people know about this," I said. "If the *Journal* finds out, you know they'll try to sabotage it. Don't even put it on the sked. Leave it off until Friday afternoon."

The sked is the daily list of stories Dow Jones reporters work on. The editors of the *Journal* see the sked in the morning and sometimes they pluck a story for the paper. But I knew if word got out to the *Journal* that I had landed an interview with Skilling, they'd try to remove me and put Rebecca on it.

Besides Jessica and Drew, four other people at Newswires knew about the Skilling interview. Heads would have rolled if the *Journal* knew we kept them in the dark about it. The *Journal* was awfully territorial when it came to Enron. They considered it their story and they hated sharing it with anyone at Newswires.

I took the red-eye to DC Thursday night and got there early Friday morning. I'd never been to the city before. I didn't sleep a wink on the flight, I was so fucking nervous. I spent those six hours practicing my own version of shorthand; Calabrese had said no tape recorders would be allowed during the interview because the government may try to subpoena any tapes as evidence.

Drew and Gene gave me a list of questions to ask Skilling. Most of them had to do with Enron's financial condition before he resigned and whether he knew about the company's off-balance sheet partnerships that were at the center of the whole scandal.

I took a cab from the airport into the city. I was fried. My face was greasy. My mouth was dry. The last time I had pulled an all-nighter was more than three years earlier, after snorting an eight ball of coke. The only thing that could keep me awake now was coffee. I went into a Starbucks and ordered five shots of espresso. It made me jittery but didn't give me the jolt I needed. It was about two degrees in DC. I still had four hours to kill before the interview.

I called Fastow's spokesman, Gordon Andrew, to tell him about the interview I landed with Skilling. I thought Fastow would reconsider if he knew Skilling was talking.

"Depends on what Skilling says," Andrew said. "Call me after you're done and fill me in."

It was too cold to take in any of the sights so I killed time at the mall. I walked over to O'Melveney and Myers. I was shaking. It wasn't the weather. It was my nerves.

The reporter from the *Houston Chronicle* was walking out of the conference room when I arrived for the interview. We nodded at one another. One of the attorneys gave me a binder filled with newspaper clippings about Skilling. She said I should use it as background information.

Bruce Hiler, Skilling's attorney—who, ironically, used to work for the Securities and Exchange Commission prosecuting people like Skilling—led me into the conference room to meet the infamous ex-CEO. I had no idea Skilling was so short. He was about five seven, and balding. How could such a short man have run such a big company, I wondered. He looked pathetic. He kept frowning, like a sad clown.

I thought he'd remember me from my work on the California energy crisis and the phone call he made to me a year earlier congratulating me on my scoop about the FERC investigation, but he said he didn't recall it.

"You got forty minutes," said Hiler, who sat in on the interview. I took a yellow legal pad from my knapsack and fired away.

"Were you aware that Andrew Fastow was benefiting financially from these secret partnerships?"

"Absolutely no idea," Skilling said, blinking his eyes at me like a puppy dog.

"What about Enron's financial condition?" I asked. "What shape was the company in when you left?"

"Absolutely, unequivocally, when I left the company August 14th I had no concern or any knowledge of problems at the company," he said, in a statement that smacked of being rehearsed. "The core wholesale business of the company had never been stronger. The third quarter earnings report was positive."

I felt like I was interrogating Skilling. I wondered if he felt nervous, like I did when I was arrested and questioned by the cops five years earlier. Hiler interrupted me a few times when I asked specific questions about Skilling's sale of Enron stock and told Skilling not to answer that question, along with several others that had to do with his role in some of the company's secret partnerships.

I got my second wind from the interview. My adrenaline was pumping. In those forty minutes I had written eleven pages of notes, more than enough for a front-page *The Wall Street Journal* story. I packed up my stuff and said goodbye to Skilling. His hand was sort of limp when I shook it. *Pathetic*, I thought. *What an act.*

I hailed a cab and headed to the Dow Jones DC bureau to write the story. I called Drew in New Jersey and told him to get ready to make history.

"Dude, he played dumb the whole time." I told Drew about Skilling's demeanor. "He said watching Enron fall apart was like watching the World Trade Center crumble."

"Nice," Drew said. "That's great color."

When the DC bureau chief found out why I was in town he was ticked off that no one told him about the interview, and pissed at me for landing it. He set me up at a desk. I took out my notes and started banging away at the keyboard like Beethoven composing a new symphony. My cell phone rang just as I finished writing the lede. It was my brother, Eric. "What's up?" I asked.

"I want you to know I just got married," he said.

"What? I mean, holy shit, congratulations."

"Thanks, we eloped," he said, "We went to a judge."

"Eric, that's great," I said, "but I'm actually in Washington, DC, right now and I'm on a deadline. I just did an interview with Jeff Skilling and I gotta finish writing it."

"Oh. Call me when you get back to L.A."

I felt bad, but at that moment I didn't give a shit about my brother's second marriage. All I cared about was this story and the look of shock on Rebecca's face when she saw my byline on it.

It only took me an hour to write, with the interview still fresh in my mind. It took Drew double the amount of time to edit it because he was so damn anal. I took a cab to the airport and got on a 6:00 p.m. flight back to L.A. I had been up for nineteen hours. I was out cold before the plane even took off.

By the time I got back to L.A. I had tons of e-mail messages from reporters I didn't even know who were assigned to cover Enron. They wanted to know how I did it—how I got the Skilling interview. If they found out, they would have strung me up and beat me like a piñata for violating the rules of journalism.

My story hit the wire hours before the *Times* and the *Chronicle* printed their Saturday papers, so a lot of media folks were under the impression that I was the only one who landed the interview.

Drew sent out the story at 8:00 p.m. Eastern time. "Ex Enron CEO Skilling Denies Role In Company's Collapse" was the headline. It was a straightforward interview in which Skilling did most of the talking. It should have been printed in the *Journal* on Monday morning, but it wasn't. Although I didn't know it at the time, Jonathan Friedland was the editor in charge of the *Journal's* Enron coverage and refused to run it in the paper.

He pointed out the story to Rebecca and John and told them to give Skilling's camp hell. John Emshwiller called Judy Leon, Skilling's DC spokeswoman, and read her the riot act for handing me the story instead of him and Rebecca. Judy called to tell me about her conversation with John.

"Emshwiller really dislikes you," Judy said. "I hate to say it, but he just went on and on about mistakes in your stories."

"I'm sorry, Judy," I said. "I don't know why he's saying those things. I don't even know the guy."

"Don't apologize," she said, "I think you should be concerned about it, though. I told John that the *Journal* could use your story and he said that I missed the point. He and Rebecca broke the story so therefore they should have done the interview."

This information fired me up, but I had no way to act on my rage. The addict in me wanted to run out and snort some lines, but I refused to let it get the best of me.

On Monday morning, the *Financial Times*, one of the *Journal*'s main competitors, printed my Skilling interview with my byline. The *Journal*'s top editors in New York yelled at Andrew Dowell for not alerting them to the interview.

"They were upset that they got scooped by the *Financial Times* from one of their own reporters," said Drew, who said he explained to the *Journal* editors that he and Gene Colter, the deputy managing editor for Newswires, told Friedland about my Skilling interview and Friedland refused to run it, so it became available to anyone else who wanted it.

"Friedland's gonna get his ass kicked," Drew said, proudly.

The following Friday I got another ACE award and fifty bucks.

ACE awards for the week ended Dec. 28, 2001

1. Jason Leopold (Los Angeles): For landing an interview with former Enron CEO Jeff Skilling.

Dow Jones Newswires was one of only three news organizations to be granted interviews with Skilling, who was making his first public remarks since Enron slid into bankruptcy proceedings. Jason's strong story from the interview was the first of the three to be published. Among other things, it was picked up by the *Financial Times*. It demonstrated his tenacity and strong desire to get the story. He flew to Washington, did the interview and wrote the story, and then almost immediately flew back to Los Angeles.

Notes like that made me feel like I had to outdo myself and continue to impress my editors. I didn't think I'd ever be able to top the Skilling story. But I did. It was a matter of being at the right place at the right time and a little bit of luck.

In January 2002, I phoned a few former Enron employees who used to work for the company's retail energy division, Enron Energy Services (EES). I was trying to find out whether any of these people knew about Enron's role in the California energy crisis. There were already rumors floating around that EES, which traded electricity in California, contributed to Enron's losses and may have been instrumental in gaming the market.

Kim Garcia, one of the EES secretaries, had been laid off from Enron in December after the company filed for bankruptcy. I called her because she was going to put me in touch with other EES employees who may have known a thing or two about the California energy crisis and if Enron had had anything to do with it.

Before we finished our conversation, Kim said she wanted to know my thoughts about a matter she'd been dwelling on for a while.

"In 1998, Enron told about seventy-five secretaries to go down to an empty trading floor and act like we were trying to sell electricity and natural gas over the phone," said Kim.

"Why would they do that?" I asked.

"'Cause they said the analysts from Wall Street were coming and they wanted to impress them."

"That sounds weird."

"Yeah, it is weird," Kim said, "'cause the phones weren't even working and the computers weren't plugged in. They told us that the analysts had to think that EES was a busy operation so we could get a good rating."

"Wait," I said. "This was for EES?"

"Yeah."

It all started to make sense. EES was set up in late 1997 to sell electricity to people who had just been freed from their local utility by newly-hatched deregulation. The big push then was signing up customers in California for retail electricity service. In 1998, EES was still a small operation, but Enron had told Wall Street that the unit was already huge and had contributed billions of dollars to the company's profits by signing up customers in California for electricity service—a lie. In reality, EES was hanging together by a thread. So Enron set up a phony trading floor, got some warm bodies down there, told them to act like they were traders, and fooled Wall Street analysts into believing that EES was a bustling operation. When the analysts returned to New York they'd advise people to buy the stock based on what they saw: that Enron was reaping the financial benefits of deregulation. Enron's stock price would go up as a result. The whole thing was a con, straight out of the movie *The Sting*. What a scam! It was brilliant.

"I think there's a story here, Kim. Don't tell this to any other reporter. I'm gonna look into it."

"I have other people you could talk to if you want."

"Great. I'll call you back in an hour or two."

It took me more than a month to investigate the story. I interviewed twenty-two former Enron employees. By the time I was finished I had uncovered the fraud within the fraud at Enron, of which Skilling was the mastermind. He, Ken Lay, EES President Lou Pai, and Thomas White, the vice president of EES who was tapped by President George Bush in May 2001 to be secretary of the army, led about one hundred Wall Street analysts around a phony trading floor. Enron spent more than half a million dollars on the charade, installing an electronic ticker tape and flat-screen monitors to give the appearance of a buzzing trading floor.

The secretaries who filled the seats were told to bring down family pictures to place on the desks to make the room look like it was lived in. Moments before Lay, Skilling, Pai, and White walked the analysts through, the secretaries got on their phones and acted like they were cutting deals. The phones were never plugged in.

But the con worked. One Wall Street analyst I spoke to who was invited to Houston to see the EES trading floor told me it looked like one of Enron's busiest operations and when he got back to New York he advised investors to load up on the company's stock.

On February 6, 2002, the story ran across the wire under the headline, "Secretaries Say Enron Had Them Pose As Traders In 1998." The first e-mail I got was from Linda Fung, the assistant managing editor for Newswires.

Jason,

The *Journal* is using your Enron story on C1 tomorrow. They just want to double check that there are no fixes coming.

Regards,
Linda Fung
Assistant Managing Editor Dow Jones Newswires

I went nuts and acted like I won the lottery. I bopped up and down in my chair like a smitten schoolgirl who had just been asked to the prom by the most popular guy in school. I started wondering whether my byline would say Dow Jones Newswires or *The Wall Street Journal* Staff Reporter. Sometimes, the *Journal* gave Newswires reporters staff writer credit because, I figured, they wanted their readers to believe that nothing got by the *Journal*. I called Drew to tell him the news.

"Dude, the *Journal* is picking up my Enron story!" I said. "Fucking C1 tomorrow."

"You're fucking amazing!" he said. "You never cease to amaze me."

Larry Ingrassia, the *Journal's* deputy managing editor, also sent an e-mail, praising the story.

Jason,

Great Enron story (I've slugged it Potemkin), which we're going to give big play to on *The Wall Street Journal's* 3rd front. Just when I think I've heard everything about Enron's machinations, yet another unbelievable thing pops up. I guarantee that it'll be one of the best-read stories in the paper tomorrow.

Kudos,
Larry

I walked into the *Journal's* newsroom the next morning to grab several copies of the paper, hoping Rebecca, Emshwiller, and Friedland would see me, but they weren't around. I seriously kicked their asses with this Enron story. I pulled out the Marketplace section of the *Journal* and right smack in the middle of the page was a beautiful bold-faced, curvy headline.

En-Ruse? Workers at Enron Say They Posed As Busy Traders To Impress Visiting Analysts
By Jason Leopold, Dow Jones Newswires

Larry Ingrassia, *The Wall Street Journal's* deputy managing editor, must have changed my lede because I didn't write the one printed in the paper. His lede was succinct and summed up the whole story: "It's not only Enron Corp's financial accounts that were phony."

I was blown away by the forty-two e-mail messages received that morning. The first one I saw was an enthusiastic note from Peter Kann, the chairman and CEO of Dow Jones & Co. An e-mail from the fucking CEO! *That's gotta mean something*, I thought. Just about every editor and dozens of reporters at the *Journal* sent emails congratulating me on the story. But the only three people I cared about, Rebecca, Emshwiller and Friedland, ignored me.

CNN, MSNBC, CNBC, *The New York Times*, and a bunch of international newspapers picked up the phony trading floor story. Reporters said it represented everything you needed to know about the culture of Enron. The *Journal* piece also summed up my own life story, especially the previous six years. In my mind, it said everything you needed to know about me. I still thought of myself as a phony and a liar and a white-collar criminal, not much different from Jeff Skilling or Andrew Fastow or Ken Lay.

National Public Radio's "Marketplace" program interviewed me alongside some heavyweights from *The New York Times, Forbes* and *Fortune* for a special broadcast on Enron called "Blind Trust."

I pushed the envelope even further on my next story. I was a news junkie who needed to go back for more. This manic behavior cost me my job.

Gordon Andrew, Fastow's spokesman, called me a week later to pitch a story. Enron had rewarded its top executives tens of millions of dollars in bonuses and stock, despite the fact that the various divisions they ran within the company failed miserably. Gordon broke down the numbers for me, which he said came directly from Fastow. I was told that it wasn't just Fastow who reaped huge financial rewards from Enron, but everyone else, too. I ran with the story. The *Journal* picked it up.

Two days later, Arden Dale got an irate phone call from a woman who represented Rebecca Mark, one of the former Enron executives profiled in the story. She said my numbers were flat-out wrong. Lawyers and spokespeople for the other former execs I wrote about, including Lou Pai and Jeff Skilling, also phoned Arden to complain about the story's inaccuracy. Fastow and his bitch really got me. Fastow's attorneys could now spin in a trial that their man was just one of many Enron executives to pocket huge amounts of cash. The only thing in the story that held up was that the five executives profiled in the story actually worked at Enron at one time or another.

Instead of coming clean and admitting that Fastow's camp duped me, I pinned the blame on Mark Palmer, Enron's spokesman. I lied to Arden and Andrew about my source's identity and never revealed that Gordon Andrew was my sole source for the story. I knew that Dow Jones would never allow me to run a story based on a conversation I had with one source, particularly one who was being prosecuted by the federal government.

When the shit hit the fan I panicked. It was like I regressed to a time when I was twelve years old and feared getting whooped by my father and so invented a huge, desperate lie. I knew it was wrong, but I allowed myself to fall prey to my irrational fears.

As a result, *The Wall Street Journal* was forced to run two retractions disguised as corrections—a total of five paragraphs long, a huge black eye for the paper. Arden called me a couple of days later and said she was taking me off Enron permanently.

"No way!" I said. "You can't take me off the story!"

"Tough," she said. "You're off. Besides, the *Journal* plans on nominating Rebecca and John for a Pulitzer and they think you're stepping on their toes. Those corrections made the *Journal* look real bad."

"Arden, I've been at this company two years and I've written close to 2,000 stories. I think I've had like five corrections total. My track record is pretty good."

"Jason, the *Journal* doesn't want you writing about Enron," she said, refusing to budge. "Move on."

"If I can't write about Enron then I have no choice," I said, "I'll have to quit."

"Do what you have to do."

I resigned from Dow Jones at the end of March 2002, a few days short of my two-year anniversary at the company. One of my coworkers told me months later that Arden planned on firing me because she and Andrew found out that I lied about my sources prior to the correction being printed in the *Journal*. My friend said that Arden knew I'd quit if she took me off the Enron beat. That's how married I was to the Enron story. In hindsight, I deeply regret the choices I made. I recognized later I had been operating like a full-blown addict; like any addict, lying was a trivial matter next to the urgent need to hold on to what I thought I needed to survive.

Two weeks before I left Dow Jones, my final story ran, one that I'd been investigating for three months about Thomas White, the former Enron Energy Services vice chairman who was then secretary of the army under President Bush. I learned from the same sources I used for the phony trading floor story that White helped cover up EES' losses when he worked there.

I was aiming my pen at the White House. I should have cut my losses while I had the chance.

ELEVEN

URGENCY TRUMPED CAUTION IN my career those days. I have the ability to be a great reporter, but then there are the stupid errors—proper names I should have double-checked, words I should have spell-checked. Or I got a word in a quote wrong because I didn't check my notes. It's been my Achilles' heel. I always wanted to be the first one out of the gate to report a story, and sometimes my errors gave other journalists the opening they needed to tear me apart.

The New York Times and the *Los Angeles Business Journal* called me after I left Dow Jones, wanting to know if I was fired as a result of the lengthy corrections that appeared in the *Journal*. Both publications were hoping to run stories about me that revolved around the corrections. The reporters dropped their stories after I convinced them that I left Dow Jones Newswires to pursue a book on the California energy crisis. Their interest in me, though negative, made me feel like some sort of celebrity with an asterisk affixed to his name.

I had a budding freelance career after I left Dow Jones thanks to my stories on the California energy crisis and Enron. I started contributing stories on both subjects to *Salon, Nation, Entrepreneur* magazine, CBS Marketwatch, and Reuters. I also agreed to help some politicians crack the

Enron case. Aides to Democratic Senator Joe Lieberman and Democratic Congressman Henry Waxman enlisted me to help the federal government pursue charges against Secretary of the Army Thomas White for his role in the Enron scandal. I willingly provided them with the names and phone numbers of my sources who could testify against White and tie him to Enron fraud.

I pursued White with a vengeance. I wrote scathing editorials for *Nation* calling for his resignation. I repeatedly placed White at the center of the fraud at Enron, based on extensive interviews with former Enron employees who worked directly with him. I tried to implicate the Bush administration in the scandal. White, being secretary of the army, was key to that component. But I didn't have the smoking gun—that is, until July 2002.

One of my Enron sources told me that several e-mails were sent to White in 2000 and early 2001 by former executives of EES warning him that EES was losing cash on many of the energy contracts it had entered into.

The controversial e-mail, which would cause this story to blow up in my face when my source was intimidated into denying, read: "Close a bigger deal. Hide the loss before the 1Q."

White had testified before a Senate committee in mid-July 2002 that EES was not a money-losing venture and that he did not mislead investors. But my sources told me that was a lie.

I phoned several other EES sources to find out whether they were aware of the e-mail White sent to a colleague saying that losses should be covered up.

Here's what one source told me: "I definitely knew of the email," the source said. "I had been told about it from my boss and others. The e-mail is definitely authentic. I heard about it from too many people for it not to be true."

This started getting interesting. I felt like I was about to outdo myself yet again.

I called another source and another—twenty-four in all—to find out exactly what the e-mails meant and to put everything into context. One of my sources, a former high-level executive at EES who had worked alongside White, explained it to me.

The exec said he had copies of energy contracts EES entered into with Eli Lilly, the Indiana-based pharmaceutical company, Owens Corning, and Quaker Oats. The contracts, all of which were signed by White, included deceptively worded details about accounting mechanisms EES used to create illusory profits. These energy contracts revealed what White knew, and when he knew it.

The Eli Lilly contract showed EES paying fifty million dollars in cash to Lilly to sign the deal. That contract also contained details of a secret partnership between Enron and Eli Lilly and showed, in black and white, that EES was nothing more than a Ponzi scheme.

The contract was worth $1.3 billion, said Enron in a 2001 press release. Documents I obtained said it was worth about 600 million dollars and if EES ever saw any money from the deal it would likely be worth little more than one hundred million dollars. The Quaker Oats contract showed how EES would book profits for doing nothing more than changing light bulbs. The Owens Corning contract contained details of another secret partnership between the two companies.

White's handiwork seemed to be all over the sixty-plus pages of documents I obtained over the course of two weeks of investigative work, including documents showing how Enron would book profits on money-losing ventures.

Several other of my sources spent a great deal of time explaining the accounting tricks the division used to book profits, and how White knew that EES was losing millions of dollars a day from energy contracts in California and other states.

This was a story for which I thought I'd win a Pulitzer. I explained the details of what I had uncovered to *Salon's* Washington bureau chief, Kerry Lauerman. I had already written five investigative pieces on Enron for *Salon* and felt a sense of loyalty to them.

Lauerman was excited, to say the least. We both felt that this story would finally show that White knew full well that the division he ran was losing tens of millions of dollars and that the energy contracts were highly suspect—and we had the documents to back it up. White, we thought, was about to go down.

I faxed the smoking-gun e-mail and the rest of the documents to Lauerman. One of my EES sources actually designed a chart on his computer so I could understand the questionable accounting practices White had employed.

I couldn't confirm the authenticity of White's e-mail with Enron because no one at the company would speak to me. So I called White's new employer, the Pentagon, and asked Major Mike Halbig, a spokesman for White, about the e-mails. Halbig told me it was time to move on, that White had already testified, and that there was nothing more to say.

"Yes, but you don't understand. I am writing a story about the e-mails, the documents, and that Secretary White told one employee to hide losses," I said. Halbig wouldn't comment.

I told that to Lauerman and he said we gave White his chance. I could simply say in my story that White refused to comment.

I had to think about this for a second. I was going up against the White House and the Pentagon, powerful institutions. I could be exposed. My felony conviction and drug use could become a matter of public record. I could be ruined. Then I thought, *I may be a felon, but White was a crook and I have proof.* I needed to chase the scoop high.

I sent documents to tax attorneys, accounting firms, analysts, and academics who helped me put accounting jargon into plain English. They all gave me the same short answer. "Wow. Enron really pushed the envelope. How did their accountants let them get away with this?"

While I wrote the story, *Salon* pored over the documents. No one had any questions.

I wasn't concerned about the authenticity of any of the documents. They all looked legit. The crucial e-mail, though, in which White tells an Enron exec to hide losses before the first quarter, didn't have any coding or headers. I supposed that it could have been doctored if someone wanted to go that far. But I trusted that it was the real thing.

Lauerman and I talked about posting all of the documents on *Salon's* website, including the e-mails, but *Salon's* managing editor said that we shouldn't give up the fruits of our labor to other reporters who could just write their own version of the story without crediting *Salon*.

Three different drafts of the story were passed back and forth via e-mail. We finally settled on a version of about 4,000 words, a good read. I felt I'd outdone myself once again. The feeling of power went straight to my head.

Salon wasn't sure when they should post the story. The Senate was still on summer break and not many politicos were in DC. We considered posting it after Labor Day but we were all worried that another news organization could scoop us if we waited too long. I didn't want to take that chance. *Salon* sat on the story for a week and decided to post it on August 29, 2002.

"Tom White Played Key Role in Covering Up Enron Losses" was the headline. It was damning. The story tied White directly to the fraud that contributed to Enron's meltdown.

When it hit cyberspace it didn't make a sound. It just sat out there. Two weeks went by. No impact. I was frustrated. I wanted some attention. I had started the biggest fire and no one seemed to notice that it was burning.

I sent copies of the story to everyone in the media and to influential government officials. *Salon* did the same thing. No one bit. No one else in the media seemed to have the balls to stand up to the Bush administration.

About two weeks after the story was published, Lauerman called me and said I should expect a call from *The New York Times* op-ed columnist Paul Krugman. He was interested in talking to me about the White story and was considering using it as the basis for one of his future columns.

"Krugman's no bullshit," Lauerman said. "So send him whatever he asks for. Any documents he wants, give to him."

"Fine. Consider it done," I said.

To Republicans, Krugman is like Saddam Hussein. If Republicans could get away with launching a war against Krugman, they would do it in a heartbeat. They hate him and everything he writes in the *Times*. He has used his column to take the Bush administration to task for its economic and foreign policies and has, on more than one occasion, called President Bush a liar. He had written about Enron's ties to the Bush administration and that the company was the largest contributor to Bush's presidential campaign. Balls. Paul Krugman had 'em.

I soon got a call from Krugman.

"My first question is why did you write this for *Salon*?" Krugman asked. "Nobody ever picks up anything from *Salon*."

I was defensive. I told him that I was loyal to *Salon*. Truth is, I had phoned the *New Republic* and some other publications about the story, but they dragged their feet.

"Well, you know this is an issue that's very dear to my heart." Krugman then asked me how I got the documents, how I cultivated my sources. I explained I had been writing about Enron and the California energy crisis for two years.

He asked me to fax him the documents. I did.

That was the beginning of a two-week correspondence with Krugman about Thomas White. He said he was planning to use my story to write his own column about White, and he'd give *Salon* and me credit. Krugman was going to make me famous. We both believed that White would be forced to resign.

Krugman asked me several questions about the substance of the documents and the e-mails and what it meant. I put him in touch with some of my sources and they answered his questions.

On September 17, 2002, Krugman's column, "Cronies in Arms," appeared in *The New York Times*' op-ed pages. The first paragraph mentioned the e-mail White wrote to one of his Enron sales execs, "Close a bigger deal. Hide the loss before the 1Q." Krugman used my name in his column. Then the shitstorm started.

My story on White had been quietly sitting in cyberspace for three weeks before Krugman got to it, while most of America's elite journalists sat on their fat asses. There are more than a thousand working journalists in the country, but in order for a story to get any kind of wide recognition it has to run in a publication like *The New York Times* or on broadcast networks like CNN. Laziness is epidemic in journalism today, and it's plagued nearly every major publication in the country.

I must have received fifty phone calls the day Krugman's column ran in the *Times*. Reporters from the *Washington Post*, ABC News, and the BBC wanted me to send them copies of my documents so they could follow up on my White story. Krugman's influence far surpassed that of *The Wall Street Journal*.

"So now you're interested," I said to more than one reporter who had the gall to call me and demand copies of my documents. Do your own goddamn digging, you lazy fucks! In all my years of reporting, I never once called another reporter to ask for his or her source material.

I did send copies of the documents to Senators Joe Lieberman and Barbara Boxer and Congressman Henry Waxman, because they promised me they would try to hold hearings that might get the White House to force White to resign once and for all.

The BBC and *ABC's World News Tonight* with Peter Jennings interviewed me about my story the day Krugman's column ran. Both networks rushed a camera crew to my neighbor's house, where I was working and had done all of the reporting on the White story.

I was unprepared for and overwhelmed by the firestorm that came about as a result of this story. It was burning out of control. *Salon* celebrated the moment. There was talk of awards.

At midnight, however, it would all come to an end, just like Cinderella.

I got a call from Lauerman.

"Jason, we've got a big problem," Lauerman said.

"What?" I said, my heart starting to beat faster. "What's the matter?"

"I got a call from an editor at the *Financial Times*," he said. "They're accusing you of plagiarizing seven paragraphs from a story they wrote earlier this year for the White piece."

Remember those stupid mistakes I mentioned? This was one of them.

I used parts of a February 2002 *Financial Times* story on suspect EES energy contracts to back up the critical points in my own story. I knew when I finished writing the White story that I hadn't yet adequately sourced the *FT*, only crediting the paper three times in my piece. But I was too concerned with getting the story done quickly and having it posted on the Internet as soon as possible, and I failed to go back and correct my mistake. Unfortunately, it wasn't the only one. I had copied down the contents of the smoking-gun e-mail incorrectly, too. I had read it so many times I thought I had it memorized. I wrote that White's e-mail said, "Close a bigger deal to hide the loss" when, according to the e-mail printout, he said, "Close a bigger deal. Hide the loss before the Q1."

Fuck. These were careless errors that I could and should have avoided. Still, no malice was intended on my part. Why would I credit the *FT*'s story a few times only to try and pass off other elements of the same story as my own work? I was stupid, but not that stupid. *Salon* probably would have run a correction and that would have been the end of it, but I had to go and put on my suit of armor and be overly defensive. I felt like they were attacking me from all sides, and I was not equipped to handle it. I resorted to what I knew. I impulsively lied. Again.

"That's bullshit! What the fuck are they talking about? I gave them credit," I shot back.

"You did," Lauerman said, "but you didn't credit them enough."

"Well, come to think of it," I said, "they stole that story from me."

I couldn't control what was coming out of my mouth, as though I were possessed.

"They did?" Lauerman asked. "Do you have a copy of your original story to prove it? I'll call up the *FT* editor and tell him."

"I'm sure I can find it in the Dow Jones database," I said.

It was bullshit. And I was knee deep in it. *FT* never stole my story. I was out of control, digging myself into a deeper grave. I called Lauerman back hours later and told him I couldn't find my original copy of the story in the Dow Jones database.

"It's a conspiracy!" I said. "Someone's out to get me."

Lauerman said Krugman should be aware of the *FT* claims. So he called him and told him about it. Krugman sent me an email after he spoke to Lauerman. He said it was no big deal.

"I should tell you that *Salon* let me know about the *FT* flap, and it's clear no harm was intended, or done," Krugman said. "I can see exactly how it happened. Someday someone will notice that the title of my book, *The Age of Diminished Expectations*, was unconsciously borrowed from Christopher Lasch."

This guy is a class act.

Salon was forced to issue a correction and I was branded a plagiarist, the worst crime a journalist can be accused of. I have never entertained the thought of ripping off another reporter's work in the course of my thirteen-year career. That was never part of my profile. I've always been determined to report the truth.

Salon didn't trust me after I lied to them. Rightfully so. Lauerman had no choice but to start scrutinizing the rest of the White story. I wasn't worried, however, because everything I wrote was supported by reams of documents.

Around this time, White had also sent a letter to the editor of *The New York Times* claiming he was unaware of any e-mails he wrote while he worked at Enron that directed an EES employee to hide losses by signing bigger contracts.

Krugman sent an e-mail, alerting me to White's letter. He said it seemed like White never even read my story, only Krugman's column.

"White has sent a pretty poor letter to the *NYT* in which he says, 'I do not recall saying or writing anything close to the quote.'" He acts as if your *Salon* article was never published, too," Krugman said.

White's letter left open the possibility that he did write the email and may have said something to the effect of hiding losses because his letter used the words "recall" and "close." But many in the media interpreted it as a vehement denial. Then they aimed their guns directly at me.

Many of the mainstream print reporters I spoke to admitted they had not read my *Salon* piece until Krugman had written about it, and some still ignored it after his column ran. But once White sent a letter to the editor at the *Times*, these reporters, none of whom had copies of my documents, started to question the authenticity of the single e-mail I attributed to White that said, "Close a bigger deal. Hide the loss before the 1Q." *Salon* was inundated with phone calls from reporters at the *Washington Post*, the *National Review*, CNN, and other major media outlets who wanted to know if the e-mail was authentic.

Lauerman called me two months after *Salon* published my story, three months after I had sent him the documents, and asked me the same questions.

"What the fuck are you talking about?" I asked Lauerman. "Of course it's real. You've had the documents for months. Look at them. White's signature is all over it."

"No, Jason," Lauerman said. "I'm talking about that single e-mail. It doesn't have any headers on it. It looks like someone typed it up on a computer and printed it out."

I didn't know it at the time, but Lauerman called my source, the person to whom White had sent the e-mail. Lauerman told my source that he'd have to go on record and corroborate the authenticity of the e-mail. When Lauerman told him that, my source froze up and denied ever speaking with me because he didn't want *Salon* to reveal his identity.

"Leopold, you fucking prick!" my source yelled at me after receiving Lauerman's call. "I'm going to sue you! I told you to keep my name out of this. Are you trying to ruin my life? I could go to jail if anyone finds out that I was involved. Your fucking editor is threatening to use my name. I told you to keep me out of it."

"I didn't know he was gonna call you," I said. "I'm sorry. I had no idea."

Lauerman proceeded to call several more of my sources to verify the veracity of the White story and the e-mail.

Some of my sources familiar with the e-mail spoke of its authenticity and even explained to Lauerman why former Enron employees won't spill details on the record.

"We don't want to get killed."

In January of 2002, Clifford Baxter, an Enron vice chairman, was found slumped over the steering wheel of his Mercedes with a single gunshot wound to the head. A suicide note was found on the passenger seat. Some former Enron employees felt certain Baxter was murdered for his knowledge of Enron's fraud, and likely murdered by former CIA or Secret Service agents employed by Enron as "security." These same sources I spoke to didn't want to get subpoenaed and be forced to testify against any former Enron executives because they feared the publicity would hinder their job search.

They all clammed up.

Lauerman demanded I send him copies of telephone bills to prove that I had spoken to my sources, specifically the person who sent me the e-mail in question.

I realized I was in deep shit, but I dealt with Lauerman with passive-aggressive behavior. I felt like I was at war. I agreed to send Lauerman my phone records, but I sat on my ass for nearly a week hiding under the covers in my apartment before I mailed them.

Lauerman wasn't satisfied. He said a record of the call I made to my source showed that I was on the phone with him for only a couple of minutes, not enough time to prove we actually had a conversation.

"You could have gotten his voicemail in that time," Lauerman said. "It's not good enough."

"But I did speak with him. He sent me the other documents, too."

That day, Lauerman got phone calls from Felicity Barringer and Howard Kurtz, media reporters for *The New York Times* and the *Washington Post*, respectively—also known as journalism's internal affairs division—who said they were going to write negative stories about me and my story based on the accusations of plagiarism by the *FT*, which were brought to their attention by White House Press Secretary Ari Fleischer.

When he called me, Lauerman was surprisingly calm.

"Jason, we're under pressure from the White House. We have to take down the White story and run a retraction."

"What? What do you mean, pressure? There's nothing wrong with my story. You can't take it down."

"We have to," he said. "Too many things went wrong."

Salon removed the Tom White story from its website two months after it was first posted and a couple of weeks after Krugman had brought it to the attention of the world.

Salon pinned the blame on me.

Oct. 1, 2002—After careful review, *Salon's* editors have decided to take down from our Web site an article titled

"Tom White played key role in covering up Enron losses" that we published on Aug. 29. We took this unusual step because we have come to the conclusion that we can no longer stand by the story in its entirety. Though we have corroborated most of the reporting in the article, some unanswered questions remain.

Specifically, we have been unable to independently confirm the authenticity of an a-mail from former Enron executive and current Army Secretary Thomas White that was quoted in the article.

Although *Salon* reviewed key supporting documents before publishing the article, we felt compelled to further investigate the story two weeks ago. At that time, we received a phone call from an editor at the *Financial Times* informing us that several paragraphs of the story, which was written by freelance writer Jason Leopold, had previously appeared in a February story in his paper.

We reviewed the complaint, discovered that it was legitimate, and posted a correction notice as soon as we were able to confirm the details. As we reported in that notice, "Leopold...told *Salon* that he accidentally copied the passages while writing his own story, and never noticed the error during the editing of the story, or after it was published."

Whatever its basis, this sort of plagiarism is a serious breach of journalistic trust, and caused us to go back over every detail and aspect of the original article. Our review led us to take this latest step.

Salon apologizes to its readers. We remain committed to upholding the highest standards of careful journalism—and, wherever questions or problems do arise, to correcting them promptly and fairly.

—The editors of *Salon*

I was a nervous wreck. I yanked strands of hair out of my head, used my thumb and forefinger to violently pluck my eyebrows, and chewed off skin from my fingertips, re-opening healed wounds from previous episodes. Once again I alienated myself from my wife and her family. I felt paralyzed and thought about suicide again.

I called Barringer at the *Times* to find out if she was really trying to pursue the negative story on me. If she did minimum homework she would discover my felony.

I put on a real sweet voice. "Hey, Felicity. It's Jason Leopold. Do you remember me? I called you like three years ago when I worked for the *Los Angeles Times* about something you wrote on *Our Times*. Remember?"

"Sorry, I don't," she said. "What's up?"

"I hear you're writing some sort of story about me? Is that true?"

"I'm not sure yet," she said. "I gotta go. I'm on deadline." She abruptly hung up.

I called Kurtz at the *Post* and left him a voicemail message but he didn't return my call.

I had one last beacon of hope, Krugman.

The week *Salon* removed the White story, Krugman called me from Tokyo to ask my help. He said his editors told him at the *Times* that if I revealed the identity of my sources, specifically the person who sent me the e-mail, then he could write a column saying he independently verified my story.

"Deal," I said. "I'll have to call them and get their permission. Give me a day."

"Okay," Krugman said, "the sooner the better."

I spent nearly twelve hours locating the twenty-four sources I used for my story. I begged them to come to my rescue.

"Please," I said, "my life is on the line here. I need you to help me."

They agreed. All of them, including the source who sent me the e-mail, as long as Krugman promised them directly that he wouldn't use their names.

"That's fine," Krugman said when I called him back in Tokyo, "I won't use their names. Let me have their phone numbers"

Krugman updated me about his progress.

"So far so good," he said in an e-mail to me, "we're getting close to the end."

Krugman also had my sources send him their income tax reports proving Enron employed them in an executive capacity and they weren't just a bunch of janitors.

On Thursday afternoon, October 3, 2002, Krugman called me at home. "We're good to go," he said. "I've verified everything. I'm gonna come out swinging in tomorrow's column."

"Paul, that's great!" I said, "You saved my life. Literally."

A couple of hours later, Krugman called back, sounding whipped.

"Bad news, Jason," Krugman said. "Can't write the column I had intended."

"Why not?"

"I'm not sure," he said, "but you're going to be getting a phone call from David Carr, a *Times* reporter. They're writing a story on you."

"You've got to be kidding"

"No. They're serious about it," he said.

"What happened?"

Krugman admitted that he would be unable to publish a column stating that he had independently verified my story.

"But Paul, my story is so on the money," I said. "Why is everyone zeroing in on this e-mail? What about all of the other documents and everything else in the story? It wasn't just a story about one e-mail. All the other documents prove White knew about the losses."

"Because the e-mail is the smoking gun," he said. "I believe you, but you went up against a very powerful person and, unfortunately, you didn't make sure everything you had was bulletproof."

"Well, why doesn't the *Times* put one of their own reporters on the story?" I asked. "You're a columnist. Why don't they get someone from their investigative team to look at this? Then they could verify everything."

"They won't budge, Jason."

I broke down and wept for a long time. I rubbed the tears away from eyes so much that the skin on my eyelids started to feel like I had a rug burn. That was the end, I thought. Soon enough, the entire world would know that I was a convicted felon and drug addict. You can't trust drug addicts and thieves. My storied career was over. I wanted to die.

David Carr called me thirty minutes later. I told him I would speak with him, but only in the company of my lawyers. My father-in-law was my attorney. He had spent the better part of the past six years bailing me out of trouble. I don't know how or why he put up with my *mishegoss*.

I called Carr back. It became clear that the *Times* was gearing up to do a hatchet job on me based on the questions Carr tossed my way. He made me so angry that I started to wonder how I could get my revenge. I went to a website that supposedly sells all kinds of shit—cow shit, dog shit, deer shit, horse shit—and wraps it up in a box with a bow and mails it to your worst enemy. I settled on elephant shit, two big logs. But ultimately, I lost my nerve.

I told Carr that he had it all wrong about me. That I was a star reporter, that I had won a journalist of the year award from Dow Jones, and that my stories on Enron caught the pleased eye of Peter Kann, the chairman of Dow Jones. If he saw copies of all those complimentary e-mails, surely he wouldn't question my character.

I put together more than thirty pages of material and faxed it to him. He called me back less than an hour later and left me a message saying he wasn't going to use any of it. While the *Times* set its sights on me for reporting what I still believe to be the truth, a rogue reporter named Jayson Blair was fabricating dozens of national news stories. The *Times* was printing many corrections and mea culpas about Blair's work during my inquisition and covering up his trail of deceit. At the same time, Judith Miller was writing a series of erroneous stories for the *Times* about Iraq concealing chemical and biological weapons that helped provoke the horrible Iraq war.

I called Lisa. "I'm finished, babe, it's over. By tomorrow the whole fucking world will know I'm a convict. I'll never work again. I think I'm gonna die."

"Jason, I love you," Lisa said. "I'm here for you. We'll get through this. We've gotten through so much together already. Don't give up on me now. Let's deal with this like a team."

On October 4, 2002, *The New York Times* ran a story by David Carr under the headline "Web Article Removed, Flaws Cited," buried inside the main section of the paper. It put a stake straight through the heart of my journalism career, and ensured that I'd never work for a major publication again. Carr basically called me a reckless journalist, untrustworthy. But then he made no mention of my felony conviction or drug use or my stint in rehab. I was floored. Maybe he hadn't checked me out.

Karen Rothmyer, my editor at the *Nation* magazine, sent me an e-mail:

> Jason: I've fielded calls from the *Times* and the *Washington City Paper* and in both cases said our relationship remains good and based on my experience I think you're a terrific reporter...I think it very likely that because of your aggressive reporting some people may have it in for you; unfortunately, you gave them an opening with that *FT* situation. It's not the end of the world. Believe me, we've all made mistakes that we remember in the middle of the night. K

I felt a little better knowing that I had some support. But that feeling quickly faded when I realized I had another problem to deal with. Carr revealed the identity of my source who sent me the Thomas White e-mail—the same source who threatened to sue me when Lauerman told him he'd reveal his identity, the same source whom I convinced to talk to Krugman by promising him that the *Times* wouldn't print his name. I immediately called Krugman and asked him to explain how it happened.

"My fault," Krugman wrote to me in an e-mail. "I am sick to my stomach. The e-mail I sent, on which you had scratched out the name, was apparently still legible. I should have marked it off better. I am incredibly sorry, and will do anything at all to help. I have clearly fucked up in earnest. Give me any lead, and I will work on trying to clear your name."

The *Times* story was contagious. On Monday, October 7, 2002, my thirty-second birthday, Howard Kurtz of the *Washington Post* put another nail in my coffin. He, too, called my credibility into question.

The media wasn't done picking at my carcass. For the next three months, *National Review, American Prospect, Washington City Paper*, and hundreds of right-wing online magazines and weblogs ran stories about Jason Leopold, the plagiarist. Robert Novak called me the "Outrage of the Week." I was nailed to the cross, tossed into the buzz saw. I had no idea what to do. I desperately wanted to fire back at my detractors, but I was outnumbered.

Then I got an e-mail from a guy named Alastair Thomps on the editor of *Scoop* (scoop.co.nz), a news site based in New Zealand—who came to my defense and talked me into writing a first-person account of what happened with me, Thomas White, *Salon*, Paul Krugman, and *The New York Times*.

"Write it as long as you want," he said. "We'll post it on *Scoop* and makes sure it gets out to everyone in the online community."

I wrote a 4,000-word story, "Shafted by *The New York Times*," that made its way around the Internet and was posted on hundreds of websites. My story was read by tens of thousands of people, and I received hundreds of e-mails of support from total strangers and best-selling authors such as Greg Palast and Mark Crispin Miller.

"Jason, your work on Enron is stellar," Palast said. "I read your story on the shafting by the *Times* and the cowardice of *Salon*. Been there, done that. The *Times* is despicable. Anything I can do to support your work let me know. I suggest you follow my professional path: Leave the country."

One alternative news publication that went by the name of mediawhoresonline.com, a website that shits on reporters who suck up to the Bush administration, even posted an "I Believe Jason Leopold" bumper sticker on its website.

The letters of praise were pretty fucking cool. I needed that kind of motivation once I crawled out of my black hole, got back on my feet, and started hammering away again.

Howell Raines, the executive editor of *The New York Times*, and Gerald Boyd, *The New York Times* managing editor, resigned in June 2003 after receiving criticism over the Jayson Blair plagiarism scandal. In 2004, the *Times* published a mea culpa, confessing that several of its stories on Iraq's alleged cache of chemical and biological weapons were flawed and based on knowledge that came from a single faulty source.

In April 2003, nearly a year after the story I wrote on him was published, Thomas White resigned his post as secretary of the army. He never gave a reason. As time went by, more evidence started to surface that supported the investigative story I wrote for *Salon* on Thomas White.

In early 2004, the Justice Department arrested Jeff Skilling and Ken Lay, charging them with a number of crimes, including instances in which they and "other senior managers and executives" concealed losses at EES—White's division—and lied to the public about the subsidiary's true financial condition.

But before that became the news that backed up my story, I freaked out. The negative press on me was taking a toll. I couldn't land a reporting gig anywhere. It felt like my arms had been amputated. I just lost it.

TWELVE

I HAVEN'T SHOWERED IN THREE days. I'm on my knees staring at the living room ceiling. My fingers are interlocked tightly. I begin to pray.

"God? Are you there?"

I press my hands to my forehead.

"I need your help. Please…kill me…I'm begging you…just take my life. Do it while I'm sleeping…I don't want to wake up in the morning anymore"

I wait, then:

"DO YOU HEAR ME, GOD? I SAID KILL ME, YOU BASTARD! COME ON, YOU PIECE OF SHIT! DO IT! FUCK YOU, GOD! FUCK YOU!"

I'm frightened of being stuck in the same room with feelings of guilt, remorse, sadness, disappointment, and heartbreak. I'm afraid these emotions, or whatever they are, will slowly kill me, and when I die, I'd prefer to go quickly. Everything I'm experiencing is too real, and makes me feel mortal. I can smell my own fear—an odor, it turns out, not unlike urine. As memories appear in my head I realize some things about myself: I'm not a tough guy; I've lost every fistfight I've been in. Hell, I've lost nearly every battle of my life: controlling drugs, keeping a job, and maintaining a sense of self after every compromise made, among them.

I walk over to the couch, crawl underneath a blanket, and turn on the television. I stay there for a week.

Lisa gives me space so I can heal. But I can't. Or won't.

She sits on the edge of the couch and puts her hand on my shoulder. It's tight, she says, and begins massaging my neck.

"How are you feeling, little baby?"

"I want to die," I say, hanging on the vowel like I'm singing it. "I can't stop thinking about everything that's happened. I wanna be numb."

"Well, you need to come up with a plan," she says. "I want you to go to a meeting."

"I don't feel like it."

"Jason, please. This affects me, too."

"I said I don't feel like going to a meeting."

Lisa gets up from the couch. She's had it. Maybe this is a moment of clarity. Maybe this is my bottom. I don't know. But I hug Lisa and say, "Okay, fine, I'll go."

A few days later I'm sitting on the therapist's couch yapping away.

"What will I do? I'm a convicted felon. How am I going to make money? Who'll hire me? I refuse to work in retail. I mean it. I am not working in retail. I want to have a baby. I want a girl. I feel like a woman. Does that make me gay? I feel fat. I hate the way I look. I have road rage. I miss my grandparents. I want a motorcycle. I want another tattoo. I want to cut myself. You think I'll be able to work in journalism again?"

Lisa's turn. "You're self-destructive and constantly test my unconditional love for you. I walk on eggshells around you."

"I never know what's going to set him off," Lisa says to the therapist.

"What do you mean by that?" I ask, annoyed.

"See. That's what I mean."

"What?

"That. The way you're speaking to me. Jason, come on. You used to jump out of the car while it was moving if I said something that upset you."

"Well I don't do that anymore, okay?"

"But you still get upset when I touch a nerve, and you don't know how to control your temper."

"Temper? I don't have a temper!"

After two months of this therapy I want out. It is too fucking hard to hear that I don't know how to have meaningful relationships. I feel cold and evil and mean after every session. Am I a sociopath? I see my father's face whenever Lisa talks about my violent outbursts, like the time I swept the pictures off the dresser in a fit of rage.

These sessions…I feel like I'm burying myself alive, but that I have to go on, for Lisa. However neutered it sounds, I know my survival depends on keeping our relationship going. I just wish the therapist could tell me when I could expect to get better.

◇

I'M JONESING FOR A story. It's been well over a month since I wrote my last piece. President Bush talks about bombing Iraq. Says the country's got weapons of mass destruction, which everyone now refers to in military-speak as WMD, and that we've got to get them before they get us. The whole country is lapping up the administration's post-9/11 jingoistic bullshit and no one's got the balls to question it. Not Congress. Not the public. And certainly not the mainstream media.

But I do. Only one problem. The publications I wrote for say I'm too great a liability and refuse to print my stories.

I go after Thomas White regardless. The story, more like an opinion piece, revels in my anger and disillusionment at Bush's war policy and the complicit media covering it.

> "Should Army Secretary Thomas White be trusted with the Army's $82 billion budget even though the division he ran at Enron contributed heavily to the company's bankruptcy and led to thousands of layoffs?"

I start thinking about Alastair at Scoop in New Zealand. Someone's gotta read this story. I send him an email. His reply comes an hour later.

"We'd been hoping you would come over to our side."

"What? You mean New Zealand?" I reply.

"No. Indie media. We're the real deal. You'll like it. We need some experienced reporters in independent media who can write hard-hitting exposés, and we'd love to run your story on White. Unfortunately, we can't pay you because we don't have a freelance budget."

In the past, independent media had a lousy reputation among major media journalists, a rep that's not totally unwarranted. Much of it was self-righteously highbrow or so poorly reported that making your way through any story felt like journeying to the center of the earth with a spoon. Journalism students are taught that the only stories with merit would be published in *The New York Times*, *The Wall Street Journal*, or the *Washington Post*. It was a fiction I bought hook, line, and sinker. Today, the mainstream media often runs half-assed stories that read more like Republican National Committee direct mail appeals. (The *Times* and *Post* eventually would finally admit that they repeated some of the Bush administration's most egregious fabrications as fact.)

I've since come to understand indie and mainstream media and the longstanding war between them. One has power and audience, the other passion and stories the mainstream media find unsuitable for a mega-corporate entity to print.

Indie media publications and websites operate largely without a broader audience and are not obligated to sell advertising space. The indie media are largely composed of hardcore journalists who care about the substance of their stories, and are actually excited about pissing off the same people who intimidate the mainstream media salary men. The old "conspiracy theory" cheap shot against indie media doesn't hold water for the public at a time when government and corporate conspiracy is revealed to be the going concern.

I may have worn a suit and tie to work in the past, but remained a head-banger at heart. As much as I've tried to fight it, I've always been drawn to those with the do-it-yourself ethos.

Publishing with indie media outlets isn't a big ego-stroker. When you're getting paid bupkis you have to question why you're doing what you're doing. My situation is a privileged one, made possible only through Lisa, who brings home our bacon.

The year 2005 signaled my comeback to significant journalism with my exclusive reports on the criminal investigation surrounding the outing of covert CIA agent Valerie Plame Wilson. My investigations hit a number of issues, like how Halliburton—the company Dick Cheney ran before become vice president—engaged in business dealings with Iraq and other rogue nations like Libya and Iran, the same countries President Bush claims sponsor terrorism.

I sounded early-warning alarms, based on little-known statements of Secretary of State Colin Powell, that the Iraq war would result in a high number of U.S. casualties if the

United States didn't get the full support of the United Nations. Those two stories, in particular, have been borne out by many subsequent reports. In 2004, one of my articles was listed as one of the top twenty-five most underreported stories of the year by Project Censored.

I've also learned that I don't need to be the first one out of the gate with a story. Today I'm slower and more cautious, adding footnotes and source material in nearly all the stories I write.

Yes, I was tossed out of the majors, but the pain that caused helped me discover who I am. All the various professional catastrophes have helped me understand that I never really came to terms with my past behavior, and as a result was never able to move forward. It's frustrating how slow it is to change. Change doesn't happen as fast as scoring a bag of coke, but it does happen.

One key milestone was the process of writing this book.

One of my biggest worries was how my parents would react. Their portrayal exposes the years of hate I felt towards them. In a nod to journalistic convention, I sent them a rough draft. I wanted them to see it first.

It was difficult: they hadn't expected the loathing inside of me; they couldn't account for my anger. But during one conversation we had after reading the book, my father surprised me.

"If this book brings you the closure you need, then you have my blessing," he said.

In other words, he loves me. I know that's his way of saying he's sorry. I'm sorry, too. I guess you could say I'm lucky.

Jason Leopold is an investigative reporter for *VICE News* who covers Guantanamo, counterterrorism, national security, human rights, open government, and civil liberties issues. He's been called a "FOIA Terrorist" by federal employees for his aggressive use of the Freedom of Information Act.